Zombies
for
Jesus

Johnny Townsend

Fic
Tow

Copyright 2010 Johnny Townsend

ISBN 978-1-60910-100-8

BookLocker.com, Inc.
2010

This book is printed on acid-free paper.

Cover design by Todd Engel

To Gertie Lou Tillotson,
for her constant love and friendship

Contents

The Ghost of Emma Smith

I was fourteen when I had my first vision. I was walking upstairs to my bedroom with a headache, intending to lie down for a half hour, but when I entered my room, there was a woman sitting on my bed wearing old-fashioned clothing. My mouth fell open, but I remembered my manners. "Hello," I said. I actually curtseyed, having watched a movie the day before where a lady did this when meeting people.

The woman on the bed smiled, raised herself up, and faded away.

I stood there in astonishment for several moments. I was terribly sleepy, but I knew I had not imagined this. I felt alert enough now to go to my parents' bedroom. My mother was taking a nap.

I shook her shoulder, and after several moments, she looked up groggily. "What is it, Eliza?"

"I think I just saw Emma Smith."

My mother sighed, and I explained what had happened. At that point, she sat up in her bed, looking worried. "Ever since we moved here in November, I've had the feeling we weren't alone. I wonder why the ghost appeared to you?" She looked at me sharply. "It certainly wasn't Emma Smith. This house isn't old enough. It was just some other woman who lived here before us. Do you suppose she's never moved on? Can a person sneak out of the Spirit World? Only resurrected people can really act as messengers, not spirits."

My family had always lived in Palmyra, and we loved staying where the Mormon Church was founded. Being

1

Mormon in Palmyra influenced everything we did or thought. We'd lived in a 1960's-era house most of my life, then one built in the 1950's, and two months ago, we'd moved into this old home built in the 1920's. It was a move up for us, a stately old house, even if in a bit of disrepair. The furnace clanked heavily, but the plumbing seemed sound, though Dad had said we'd need to replace the hot water heater soon. We eventually wanted to find a house that had actually been around back in 1830, but those were hard to find and very expensive. My mother was the driving force behind our going backward to older and older houses. My father would sigh whenever my mother found a new prospect, but he liked antiques and seemed to want the simpler way of life an old house represented, so he went along with the moves.

"I know why she appeared to me," I said timidly.

"Now, I won't have any more of that, Eliza."

I nodded and went back to my room. I knew, though, that it was time for a new direction in the Church. I'd read the Book of Mormon and the Doctrine and Covenants and parts of the Bible. Women might be the mothers of nations, the mothers of prophets, of the Messiah himself, but they were still afterthoughts. I realized, however, that it was time for a woman to become a prophet. I was fourteen now, the same age Joseph Smith had been, and in the same town he had lived in, when he had his first vision. I knew it was my destiny.

The fact that it was Emma Smith who had appeared to me, and not Adam or Moroni or Peter, told me I was right.

I knelt beside my bed and prayed. "Heavenly Father, I'm ready. Please send Emma back to me."

I stayed on my knees half an hour and eventually grew tired and fell asleep on the floor beside my bed.

Over the next several days, I continued to feel the presence of an unseen being. I began talking to her when I was alone, in case she could hear me. It seemed to happen most often in the late evening or early morning. At school, there was no hint of prophetic inspiration. I couldn't even pass my algebra tests. And in the afternoon when I came home, I felt completely alone in my room. It was only as the evening dragged on into the late hours that I could feel Emma trying to reach me again.

One Saturday, when I was in the kitchen with Mom, my little brother Samuel came up to us. "What do you want, Mom?"

She looked at him and laughed. "What do you mean?"

"I heard you calling and calling."

Mom looked at me and then back at Samuel. "No one's been calling you, dear."

"Sure you were."

"I've been here all along," I offered. "Mom never called."

Samuel stomped his foot. "Real funny," he said and stormed off.

Mom looked at me quizzically, but I looked away, irritated. Had Emma Smith been calling to Samuel? Was I being passed over for yet another male? Had I done something wrong? Not displayed enough faith? Samuel was only eleven. It seemed very unfair for him to get to be a prophet.

My headaches seemed worse over the weekend, though I usually felt better after getting out of the house for a few hours on Sunday for church. I began hearing bells ringing in the middle of the night, and once I woke up with the vivid sensation that someone was strangling me. I fought off the attacker and turned on my lamp, only to find the room empty.

I felt a chill run through me. I remembered that just before Joseph Smith's first vision, he was attacked by unseen hands, too. I was happy to know I was still being considered for the position of prophetess, but a little unnerved as well.

One evening during dinner, when the whole family was around the kitchen table, there was not much talking, unusual for us. Everybody seemed to be in a bad mood or depressed or feeling nauseated. I had lost my appetite but was forcing myself to eat because I knew my mother always worked hard on dinner.

"The green beans came out really good," I said.

Mom nodded listlessly.

I looked at my brother. "Sam, what did you study in English today?"

"We read a story about ghosts," he said glumly. "I told my teacher we had ghosts in our house, and she gave me punishwork to do."

"Well, we certainly don't have ghosts," said my Dad firmly. "Don't be ridiculous."

"Doesn't the Church teach that our spirits go on after we die?" I asked. "Why can't there be ghosts?"

"Spirits go to the Spirit World or Spirit Prison after they die," said my mother. "They don't hang around here."

"But you said—"

My mother shook her head at me sharply.

"I saw a woman in my room," said Samuel.

"You most certainly did not," my father replied.

"Joseph Smith saw ghosts," I offered.

Mother put her fork down and looked at my father nervously. "He did not. He saw resurrected beings. There's a big difference." I looked at my father, who was rolling his eyes. It irritated me.

"But they were still dead people," I insisted. "I think Emma Smith has been coming here. *I* saw her once, too." I looked at my brother for confirmation. He was staring at his plate queasily.

"I won't tolerate another word on the subject," said my father. "I—"

"Do you hear that?" I interrupted, holding out my hand over the table to shush everyone.

"What?"

"Footsteps upstairs!"

Everyone listened. "I don't hear a thing."

"It's as plain as your snoring at night. And it's coming from my room!" I jumped up from the table and hurtled up the stairs two at a time. I threw open the door to my room and looked about.

My father and mother were right behind me. "Well?" demanded my father.

"I don't see her," I said in disappointment. "But I'm sure that—"

"Oh, good grief. The Church has poisoned you with all this nonsense. There are no prophets, no visions, not even any Spirit World. It's all superstition."

"Oh, Mark, how can you say such a thing?"

"Dad, you're going to get us zapped. We'll all die in our sleep."

"Anybody up here?" asked Samuel.

"No. We're going back downstairs to finish our dinner."

"I'm not hungry."

"Get back downstairs."

Maybe my Dad was the reason Emma was hesitant in appearing to me. Joseph Smith had had supportive parents, and even a prophet needs support if he's only fourteen. I had to convince Emma to come see me even if my father was an apostate.

I left little notes for Emma in my room the next day, and I fasted on Friday. Saturday morning, I read more of a biography on Emma, and Saturday afternoon while I was praying for God to call upon me, I fell asleep beside my bed.

I woke up later with a splitting headache, and my vision was a little blurry. But I could distinctly feel someone else was in the room with me.

"Emma?" I asked.

I heard a rustling and stood up to look around. Right in front of my dresser was a woman. I couldn't tell if it was the same person I'd seen before, but I started walking toward her, smiling. She began walking toward me as well.

"What can you tell me?" I asked. "What's the revelation? My news for the world?"

There was no response, and I stopped walking. Emma did, too. Then as my vision cleared, I saw that I was looking at my reflection in the mirror. Had it all been a mistake?

I shook my head. I was *sure* there had been someone else in the room. Perhaps when I stopped walking toward her, I demonstrated a lack of faith and made her disappear. Why hadn't I gone up to embrace her?

Sunday, Dad said he felt too sick to go to church, but we all suspected that after his confession of faithlessness, he was just trying to avoid taking the sacrament. I couldn't do a complete fast again so soon, but I skipped breakfast, asking for God to touch my father's heart, and to send Emma back to me again. Maybe Emma could tell me how I could reach into my father's soul. Saving my own family would be as important as anything I could do for the Church.

I confided in my friend Shelly after Sunday School what had been happening. I tried not to be obnoxious about my privileged status, but I still expected her to be impressed.

She was not.

"Oh, Eliza! That house is haunted. I meant to tell you when you moved in, but I didn't want to scare you. The family that lived there before all reported seeing and hearing strange things, and then one day they were all found dead in their beds. You've got to get out of there."

I was dumbfounded. Could Shelly be right? We were told that Satan could appear as an angel of light. Were these evil spirits in our house and not good ones? Was I really not about to be chosen as a prophet? Maybe the woman in my room was the wife of one of the early persecutors.

Still, I thought, if I was in tune enough with the Spirit World to see this much, I could ask for more. I could still see Emma if my heart was pure.

I went to my Dad's bedside after I returned home and put my hand on his head. He smiled weakly. "Hi, honey."

"Still feeling rotten?"

"I have a terrible headache."

I hesitated a moment and then blurted out, "I know I don't have the priesthood, but I can still give you a blessing."

Dad frowned.

"I've seen Emma Smith twice now. I can ask her to see that you're healed. On the other side, I bet women *do* hold the priesthood. I think—"

Dad forced himself to sit up. "Eliza, I'm going to have to forbid you to ever go back to church."

"What?"

"I thought it would be harmless to let kids have some socializing outside of school. But I can see these toxic teachings just go on seeping insidiously into your brain."

"Dad, it's all true. Emma—"

"I'm taking away your Church books. From now on, you'll read classics, or science books, or history books."

"My biography of Emma is a history book."

"That does it."

Dad swung his legs to the floor and stood up in his underwear. He wore just boxers and a T-shirt, not the special garments Mom wore after they went through the temple. It made me sad to see him so decadently secular.

Dad headed toward my room, and I suddenly realized what he was up to. "No, Dad!" I said. "You can't. The Church is good. The Church is true. I'm going to be a prophet. I—"

Dad pushed open my door and walked into the room, with me only a step behind. He stopped abruptly and stared at my dresser. I frowned.

"Oh, my god."

"What?"

"There's a woman in your room."

Now my *Dad* was having a vision? My heart started beating faster. *He* wasn't going to steal my revelations away from me, was he? I remembered that Paul and Alma the Younger and the sons of Mosiah had all been wicked and then seen miraculous visions and become great men.

It wasn't *fair*. I was the one who was always good. I was the one the Church needed. Why were men always chosen over women? I stomped my foot.

"Emma!" I called. "I want you to appear to me right now!"

My father collapsed on the floor, and I reached down to revive him. There was no response. It was just like King Lamoni. I ran to get my mother. She called an ambulance, and soon we were all at the hospital awaiting word. Had my father been struck down like Korihor for doubting? Were we going to lose him? Perhaps his illness was just to provide a way for me to show the power of women when I healed him later.

After a long while, the doctor came over to us, smiling grimly. "It looks like your husband is suffering carbon monoxide poisoning. I expect you all are. You'll have to leave your home until you can get it checked out and repair whatever gas appliances are causing the problem."

My mouth fell open.

"Have you been experiencing headaches?" the doctor went on. "Hearing noises? Seeing things?"

I closed my mouth and could feel my jaw clench. This man was *not* going to take away my visions. It was a lie, a tool of the devil to shake my faith. If I proved myself strong now, I could still earn my place among the prophets.

"Do you have somewhere to stay?" asked the doctor.

"Yes," said my mother. "We're friendly with the neighbors next door."

"Good. But first, let's see if we need to admit any of the rest of you to the hospital as well."

We submitted to the blood tests, and before long, we heard the verdict. My mother would have to stay in the hospital at least overnight while receiving pure oxygen. Samuel and I had to breathe it for a couple of hours, but we were allowed to go to the neighbors' house as long as we came back for another dose of oxygen tomorrow.

Mom called Mrs. Thompson, who agreed to come pick us up. Samuel and I had dinner with them, and then we were ushered off to bed, Sam sharing her son Allen's room, since Allen was in Sam's class at school, and me getting the guest room all to myself.

Lying in bed in the dark, I thought about what to do. Even if it were true that my visions were caused by carbon monoxide, I had to wonder if that wasn't a viable catalyst for enlightenment, like peyote or LSD or any of the other things people used. Emma hadn't been a hallucination. I had truly seen her. And I wanted to see her again.

After the Thompsons were finally asleep, I put on my shoes and slipped out the back door. It was especially cold tonight, and I wanted to make sure to get enough gas to compensate for several hours out of the house, so I turned up the furnace. It was like seeding a cloud, I decided. Joan of Arc might have been schizophrenic to receive her visions, but she was still a prophet, even if not recognized by the Church. For all I knew, Joseph Smith had been bipolar or schizophrenic himself. But that didn't keep him from being one of the greatest prophets of all time. So maybe I simply needed carbon monoxide to put me in tune with God.

But I *was* going to do it. I was going to be a prophet.

I opened the vent in my bedroom more fully, knelt beside my bed, and started praying.

I prayed longer and harder than I'd ever prayed before. I swore eternal chastity, vowed to raise eight children, promised to serve eighteen months as a missionary, said I'd finally finish reading the Bible. I explained why I felt it was so important to finally get a woman's perspective in the Church, though I insisted I would follow whatever advice was revealed to me. I committed myself to ensuring the continual growth of the gospel and the obedience of the saints.

"Nothing is more important to me than being useful to the Church," I prayed aloud. "I can make a difference. I can. Please use me."

After three hours on my knees, though, I discovered Satan trying to sneak his way into my mind. Letting myself be poisoned was reckless. If I could only lead the righteous through brain damage, perhaps there was something wrong with the righteous as well. Maybe no one throughout history had ever seen God. Perhaps every vision ever recorded was a simple matter of brain chemistry.

I decided to get up and go back next door. But it was late and I was so very tired. I stretched out my legs and leaned against the side of the bed. Just a quick nap and I'd go downstairs and leave the house.

I'd study Joseph Smith's visions and those of others more carefully. Maybe it was all still true. And if it was, I'd manage to find a way to join their ranks. But it was too late to worry about that now. I needed to rest my heavy eyelids for just a moment.

I closed my eyes. The house felt so warm and comfortable.

"Eliza."

"Eliza."

I opened my eyes. Emma Smith was standing before me.

"You must leave this house immediately. There are important things in your future."

"Really?"

"Get up and go."

I stood beside the bed, holding onto it for a moment to catch my balance. When I looked up, Emma was gone.

But she'd spoken to me this time, which she hadn't done before.

I walked down the stairs and back to the Thompsons' house. I fell asleep almost immediately, and I had a terrible headache when I awoke in the morning.

We had our furnace repaired, and the headaches and queasiness and footsteps and voices and visions stopped. I never saw Emma Smith again, and I never knew if that last vision of her was real or not. I gave a long talk on Emma in church one day, and a report on carbon monoxide in science class, and eventually I graduated both from high school and from Seminary class.

I did go on to serve a mission, and marry in the temple, and have two children of my own.

But I never did have another revelation. My father eventually stopped going to church, and even had his name removed from the records. Samuel also stopped his church attendance, never even going on a mission as I had. Mom died last year, still active in the Church.

I miss those early days in our last house, the joy and wonderment mixed with the headaches and nausea. But I have carbon monoxide detectors in my own home now, and neither of my two daughters has ever seen a vision. I'm not sure if I'm doing them a favor or not. I hope one of them will be a prophet one day, but only if their visions are real.

If such things actually exist to begin with.

I have a painting of Emma Smith on my bedroom wall. I look at it often and hope.

Nursing Wounds

I won't call him, Miranda told herself firmly. It was Keith's birthday, but she would *not* call him. That would show him. He always thought she'd just jump at his beck and call. Well, now he'd see.

Miranda opened her pharmacology book and started reading the chapter assigned for tomorrow. She was already tired from all the day's classes, and it seemed pointless to study, if she and Keith were breaking up. He was the whole reason she was in nursing school to begin with. He'd been working here at Charity when they first started dating, God, was it six years ago? That was back just before he got his divorce, back when both he and Miranda were renting rooms in the home of the Robertsons, that awful family in their Mormon congregation. Miranda was sure he'd marry her after the divorce, since they'd been having sex, but he said he needed time to adjust.

She'd granted it, but a year later, he still wasn't ready. Then he began complaining that the reason was her salary as a receptionist. He wanted her to make as much money as he did. She knew then that he was selfish, and she realized his first wife had paid for his nursing school, and that now he'd still expect Miranda to give him money. But she did need a better career, and so after another year of badgering, she'd enrolled at Delgado to start earning her pre-nursing credits part-time while still keeping her day job.

Things were rocky by then, with Keith always yelling at her or telling her he was seeing other women, but she knew he must really love her because he was always coming back to her in the end. He said it was just because he wanted sex and liked her "voluptuous" breasts, and it was of course true that he almost always started tearing her clothes off as soon as she came in the door, but Miranda knew. He was so handsome he could have any woman he wanted. Miranda had even seen him with pretty women, one a doctor, and another black, and since Miranda was getting fatter every day, he couldn't keep wanting to have sex with her unless he really loved her.

Last night, though, he'd said he didn't love her. "If you ever come over again, I'll hurt you. I swear it. Don't ever call me again."

"But you're the one who calls *me*."

He'd just glared. "I swear I'll hurt you." He did have a few guns, and Miranda had given him a hunting knife on his last birthday, but if he was going to be such an asshole, she wouldn't even call him today on this birthday. She'd wait until *he* called. It might take another couple of weeks. It always took two weeks after they argued, but it was always Keith who called first. Almost always, anyway.

Miranda looked again at her textbook. She was making mostly C's and B's now in her first semester of nursing school. Keith had promised to help her study but never did. He only yelled at her when she made C's. "You're so stupid. How do you ever expect to become a nurse? Who would hire you anyway?" But he only said it because he was jealous. He'd failed a couple of courses when he first started out, and had had to go to another school.

So she'd study without him. She'd show him. She'd be a nurse and make as much as he did, and then he'd sure want her.

Miranda read for the next ninety minutes, highlighting parts she knew she'd need to remember. It was 7:30 now, time to eat again, but she still had so much studying left for her other classes. If Keith called and asked her to come over, she could honestly tell him she just didn't have time for him today.

But she did need a break. She stood up and listened at her door. She didn't hear anyone, but that Xiomara was somehow always ready to jump out of her room whenever Miranda opened her door. Xiomara liked to borrow clothes, or money, or food, or to yap and yap about her doctor boyfriend. If she had a doctor boyfriend, though, Miranda certainly didn't know why she made such an effort to break up her relationship with Keith. Miranda wasn't sure if she just wanted Keith for herself, or if she simply wanted to cause misery in other people's lives for its own benefit. Maybe that was why Xiomara was studying nursing. She just wanted to be around sick, miserable people, and maybe make them a little more miserable. Of course, she was doing so poorly she'd probably never become a nurse anyway.

Smiling slightly, almost defiantly, Miranda opened her door and quietly headed down the hallway toward the kitchen. She moved two dirty pots to the sink and then heated up a Libby's meal in the microwave. She had just sat down to eat when she heard some girls walking down the hall and giggling.

They were moving away, so they'd probably already passed the kitchen and peeked in. They were surely laughing about her. Well, it was true—she was fat, a size fourteen now, though she'd been a nine when she first met Keith. She didn't need to be eating this stuff with all its fat content, but she didn't have time to prepare a good meal. Those girls were still young. They'd be fat, too, by the time they were thirty-one.

Miranda continued eating as she heard the elevator doors close and the giggling ceased. Now they'd be telling the elevator lady about how Miranda was stuffing her face again.

She knew they told stories about her all the time. Why else would the elevator lady always be scowling at her? The woman didn't scowl at anyone else. Just her. People *must* be saying bad things about her.

Miranda washed her spoon and threw her used container away. Last week, the floor captain had yelled at her for leaving dirty dishes in the kitchen. They weren't Miranda's, though, not most of them, and she'd vowed not to even use any dishes until the captain realized it.

Miranda slipped back to her room unnoticed by Xiomara and closed the door gratefully behind her. Then she opened a bag of pretzels and munched on them as she read her chapter in Nutrition.

She kept glancing at her clock as she reached the bottom of each page, but Keith still hadn't called yet. She was getting mad by 9:00 when he *still* hadn't called. The nerve! He was always trying to do exactly what he thought she'd hate most. But two could play at that game.

Last month, for instance, when she'd refused again to let him do anal sex to her, and when he'd insisted for the first time that she put her finger inside of him, which of course she'd also refused, he'd yelled at her. "Everyone else does this! Why do you always have to be Miss Purity? Other girls let me fuck them in the ass. If you want to keep seeing me, you'd better loosen up."

"Why *do* you keep seeing me then?" she'd asked, knowing that the answer was that he loved her, but hoping to trick him into saying it. "I don't do that other thing you like either," meaning, naturally, oral sex. He kept insisting she let him come in her mouth, but the very idea nauseated her. She'd forced

17

herself to try a couple of times, but she'd gagged and had run to the bathroom, and he'd yelled and yelled at her about that, too.

"You're not very proficient, you know," he went on. "Other girls do this all the time. I don't know why I even waste my time on you."

"Why *do* you?" she repeated.

He'd glared at her. "It's not because of what you think!" he hissed.

"What do I think?"

"You know what you think. It's not because of that. I'll never love you. I'm just horny tonight. That's all there is to it."

"But you say you could get any girl. You say you're already dating several girls." Why couldn't he just admit it? Things would be so much simpler if he could just admit he loved her. They'd be able to work through all the rest.

"Get out," he said. "I don't want to ever see you again. Get out!" He shoved her off the bed and threw her clothes at her, cursing and screaming as she sobbed while getting dressed.

But even then, she knew he still loved her. They always had a few good days before a bad one. They'd wait a couple of weeks, have a few more good days, and then another bad one. If she could just get him to admit how he really felt about her, there wouldn't have to be any more bad ones at all.

Two weeks after the last anal sex attempt, about two weeks ago, she'd called him again. He was very distant, so she knew someone was there with him. "Are you alone?" she'd asked.

"I'm fucking someone else right now," he'd said and hung up.

Would he really have said that if another girl were right beside him? Yes, he would. Just to make Miranda mad. They were probably in bed that very moment laughing about her. Miranda was so upset, she called right back and hung up as soon as Keith said hello. Then she kept calling back every ten or fifteen minutes until 2:00 in the morning, always hanging up.

Finally, Keith picked up the phone and hissed, "You bitch" before Miranda could hang up. But she didn't call back any more that night.

Miranda smiled. It was Keith who called last night, though, asking her, no, *begging* her, to come over. And like always, he started ripping her clothes off as soon as she walked in the apartment, tying her up as usual, and having sex without a condom. He always pulled out just before he came, since four or five times in the past six years Miranda had told him she thought she was pregnant. She did hope to get pregnant and so didn't mind that he wouldn't wear a condom. He'd surely marry her if she was pregnant. He'd left his wife with a baby, but that was different. He loved Miranda. Wasn't that why he wouldn't use a condom? He couldn't admit he loved her, but he *wanted* her to get pregnant so he could say that was the reason he married her.

He'd finally take her out in public then. He wouldn't have to be afraid of what people at church thought. That was why he got mad all the time, because Miranda had told the bishop about their affair years ago, back when she believed in the Church and thought she needed to repent. But then he'd denied everything, and the bishop had believed *him*. Now Keith was always accusing her of telling on him, though she hadn't even been to church in three or four years now.

When they had sex, if she reacted too slowly, he'd accuse her of not liking it, which was sort of true, but she couldn't let him know that. Instead, he went on accusing, "Are you going to tell the bishop how I did this?" And he'd lick her breasts. "Or how I did this?" And he'd lick her private area. "Or how I did this?" And he'd ram himself inside her so quickly that it hurt. Then she had to pretend she liked it so he wouldn't be afraid she was going to tell on him.

Last night, he'd called her after 10:00, and she'd gone right over. After he pulled out, she said, "It doesn't matter. I think I'm already pregnant." It wasn't true. She'd had her period last week, but she just felt like saying it. She wasn't even sure why.

"God damn." He turned her over and tried to get inside her. "You're going to take it up the ass from now on. If you don't want to, I've got some drugs I can give you." He crawled over to the side of the bed and opened a drawer, pulling out a hypodermic and a vial.

"No!" she said. Was he crazy? What *was* that?

"And if you're pregnant, you're going to have an abortion," he said coldly, staring levelly at her, and she knew it was coming, "just like last time."

"No!" Miranda had cried, unable to stop herself. The pain of that terrible loss, always lurking around inside, had burst back out. "I never had an abortion! I had a miscarriage! A miscarriage!"

"That's not what Eric tells me."

Men! Everyone always believed men. Eric had dumped her when she became pregnant eight years ago, and when she'd had a miscarriage a month later, he'd told everyone he'd left her because she'd had an abortion. Keith and Eric had grown up together, but Keith knew it was a lie. Miranda was sure he believed her. How could he dare say such a horrible, horrible thing?

And Miranda still knew Keith wanted her to be pregnant. Hadn't that been her birthday present four months ago? When they'd had sex that day, he hadn't pulled out. He'd come inside her and said, "Happy Birthday."

Keith lifted the hypodermic and brought it closer. "No! I'm not pregnant. I just said it to make you mad."

Keith carefully put the hypodermic back in the drawer, and Miranda turned over again onto her back, but he jumped on top of her and flipped her onto her stomach again. "You're going to take it, and you're going to like it!" Her hands were still tied above her head, so there was little she could do.

"No. Please. No!"

He tried just a moment more and then shoved her back over. She was crying. "If you ever come over again, I'll hurt you," he said in a monotone. "I swear it." He let her dress, and she left, still sobbing.

But today was his birthday. Wouldn't it hurt his feelings if she didn't call? She knew he could be nice and sweet if only he'd let himself. And she could help him. She knew she could. If only he'd say he loved her, if only he'd stop worrying about the people at church, if only he'd just realize how good they could be together, everything would be fine. If he still kept seeing her after six years, their relationship *must* be okay. They'd already been together longer than he'd been with his wife. If he could just see how faithful Miranda had been, how he didn't have to worry, things could be really good. And if she didn't call him on his birthday, how could he know that? She'd have to call.

But she wouldn't. He deserved to be shaken up a little bit. Maybe then he wouldn't take her for granted so much. It was getting close to 10:00. He'd call and ask her over, and she'd say she already had a date. He was going to have to start appreciating her a little bit more.

Miranda picked up a notebook and began reading the notes she'd taken in class, but her mind just wouldn't cooperate. She found herself staring at the clock for several minutes at a time.

Maybe, she thought, maybe she should give him a special birthday present like he gave her. Maybe… she shook her head. She could never take his cum in her mouth, but maybe… maybe she could let him do anal sex to her after all, even if she did have to be drugged first. Then he'd realize she did love him, and maybe then he'd be able to admit he loved her, too.

But *he'd* have to be the one who called. If he called, then she'd do it, but she wasn't going to go crawling to him any more.

Smiling, she picked up her notebook again and read through the last two lectures. It all seemed finally to be falling into place. She ought to make a high B on her next test. Maybe even an A.

But then she looked at the clock again. It was 11:30. "Damn!" She was sick of studying by now but had to keep her mind occupied. She started reading her notes again. "I will not call him. I will not call him," she chanted softly as she read. He was going to have to make the first move. It was hard to resist, but he wasn't going to be able to tell everyone she was after him. He had to *admit* he wanted her.

But it was 11:45. What if she called and he wasn't even home? What if he was in bed with another woman?

No. She knew he was just waiting for her. It was all simply a power struggle. He loved her. She knew it, and he knew it. But he was going to have to call first.

It was 11:50. Only ten more minutes left to his birthday. It was the first time in six years she hadn't given him a present. And she would have given him one this time, one better than any of the others. If he was too proud and stubborn, well, that was his loss.

11:55. Oh, my god, why wouldn't he call? It was like playing Chicken. How close could the two cars get before one ran off the road? She stared at the phone. Well, she wasn't going to run off. She wasn't.

Then she had an idea. She could call and just hang up. Yes! Then he'd have to call her right back, and *then* they'd talk. Oh, it would work perfectly. He'd still be the one to call. Why hadn't she thought of it earlier? Her 9:00 class was going to be hell in the morning now.

She breathed deeply, picked up the phone, and dialed.

Murderers of Old Men

It was Rick and Nancy's twentieth wedding anniversary. Things had been a little dull the past few years, but their oldest son, Ted, had just entered the Missionary Training Center the week before to prepare for his mission to Guatemala. That ought to give them something more to talk about over dinner. Really, it would be a relief to have the boy out of the house. He had signed up for only two courses each semester at the university this past year, just enough to justify not having to work. But rather than study, he'd spent most of his afternoons listening to music and playing his guitar. He didn't even claim any special talent that would miraculously lead to superstardom. He simply vegetated in his room every day, wasting away. Surely, being transplanted to Guatemala would be good for him, even if the boy had only agreed to go because Rick promised to buy him a car if he stayed the full two years.

Ted wouldn't even volunteer for three hours on a Saturday to help plant trees with the Urban Tree Project, one of Rick's favorite charities. Rick enjoyed filling the downtown and suburban roadways with more greenery, but Ted just shrugged and said, "Two years is plenty of service. I don't have to give up my whole life, do I?"

Rick and Nancy were planning to leave their two girls at home this evening and head out for a dinner at Applebee's. They'd tried TGIFriday's once and actually preferred it, but they couldn't bring themselves to go back to a restaurant that took the Lord's name in vain.

Rick left work early so they wouldn't be rushed. Sex was a real possibility on his anniversary if he didn't louse things up.

Maybe even an actual smile or two. Rick's cell phone buzzed as he pulled onto the freeway. After a quick glance to make sure no police were nearby, he answered.

"Rick. This is your dad." Rick's father never called. Rick hardly ever called him, either. Not since the man had divorced Rick's mother two years ago.

"Hey there. What's up?"

"Gramps is dead."

"Oh, no." Rick's grandfather was 101 and had been in good health. But at that age, what could you expect?

"He was murdered this morning."

Rick almost dropped the phone. "What?"

"He and another man from the nursing home were killed. They were at the funeral of a friend of theirs, and someone actually came out and shot them. Apparently, the woman who'd died had been fooling around with some of the men at the home, and her husband just shot all the guys who showed up."

"I can't believe it." His first thought was of the jovial old man he visited once a month. But his second thought was of the dead woman. There were women in their 90's who still had sex?

"The other man killed was 99. And another guy who was hurt was 100."

Rick remembered all the genealogy he'd done in his life, looking at countless gravestones. He realized that in the future someone would look back at his grandfather's marker and just assume he'd led a good, long life and had died of natural causes. They wouldn't understand that this was wrong, that he'd been cut down early, that this was an atrocity.

"Good grief, Dad. When's the funeral?"

"The wake will be tomorrow, and the funeral is Friday at 11:00. Can you and Nancy make it?"

"Of course, Dad."

Rick saw a police car in his rearview mirror and hung up. He drove the rest of the way home in a daze. When he pulled up to the house, Nancy was out front watering the lawn. She looked as if she was crying. Rick was a little surprised, since while he himself liked Gramps well enough, Nancy had never been particularly close to him.

"So you heard?" he asked, stepping out of the car.

"Heard? I can *see*! Look what they've done!"

It wasn't till that moment that Rick saw the reason Nancy was watering. Half the lawn and almost all the shrubs were clearly dying, obviously beyond hope despite the water.

"What happened?" Rick asked, confused.

"Some kids, probably," said Nancy, sniffing. "They've poured herbicide all over my roses, all over my peonies, on the oak, and they've hit half the lawns on this street." Rick remembered hearing on the evening news about these awful vandals, who had already hit five other neighborhoods in the city over the past couple of months. "They're killers! Murderers! And I hate them!"

This quickly brought Rick back to the news he had to share, and when he told Nancy, she sat down on the wet, dead grass and cried. They weren't allowed to call Ted in the MTC, but Rick sent him a quick email the boy could read on Preparation Day. The girls were home a few minutes later, and he told them about the killing as gently as he could.

"Better than dying of cancer," said Shelly.

"Better than having Alzheimer's," said Karen.

"But worse than dying in your sleep when *God* decided it was your time to go, not some evil man."

"Whatever."

Rick took a shower and got dressed for the evening. Nancy was still sniffling but didn't want to miss out on dinner. Rick only took her out maybe four or five times a year. He'd thought for a while that she might be more willing to offer sex if he treated her to a nice meal, but he felt that really turned her into a prostitute. However, he was willing to try just about anything. After a few years of monthly restaurant excursions and only bimonthly sex, though, he'd given it up. Nancy was expecting a movie tonight after Applebee's, but since she always complained that Rick didn't talk enough, he had conversation planned not only during dinner but afterward, too. He'd made out note cards and prepared for this as he would any presentation at work. He was determined to have sex again. It had been almost three months. He felt lifeless without it. Rick would have to wing the presentation tonight, though, without the help of Power Point.

As they walked out to the car, Nancy looked at the yard, and her shoulders slumped. Rick was angry about the ten-year-old rose bushes, but when he looked at the oak and knew it only had days left, he felt downright sick. That tree was already eighty years old, planted when this house was first built. How could someone so casually kill such a majestic life?

Driving to Applebee's, Rick thought of the Redwood League he'd donated $50 to a couple of weeks earlier. This wasn't on his note cards, but he decided to add it to the conversation. "Do you think we should get flowers for Gramps' funeral, or should I donate to a charity in his name?"

"Did he have any favorite charities?"

"Just the ladies. You know, like Dad."

"So what kind of charity were you thinking of?"

"Something that will leave a legacy."

"Like what? He was already a walking sperm clinic."

The phrase was clearly meant to be cutting, but it made Rick feel sorry for his Dad for the first time, and to feel sorry for his grandfather. Life always wanted to go on, didn't it? Even old men wanted to spread their seed.

"I was thinking of something along the lines of Save the Redwoods League."

Nancy sighed heavily. "Oh, you and your trees. This is supposed to be to honor *him*, not to appease your own interests."

"In the Book of Mormon, the people were commanded to let all the trees grow and not cut any down, because they had abused nature too much."

"So saving the Redwoods is commanded in the Book of Mormon? You're doing this because your grandfather was so dedicated to the scriptures?"

Rick realized that Nancy knew darn well Gramps had never read the Book of Mormon even once. He'd never gone on a mission, though he did marry in the temple. Still, he'd hardly been to church in ten years. The closer he got to death, the less interested he seemed in the afterlife.

"No one benefits from seeing $75 worth of cut flowers for one day. Everyone should give to charity at every funeral, no matter which charities they choose."

"The family benefits from the flowers. It makes them feel someone cared."

"And do Karen and Shelly care?"

"You have to show care for them."

They arrived at Applebee's a couple of minutes later and went inside. Since it was a Wednesday, there was not a large crowd, and they were seated within five minutes. Nancy ordered veal, and Rick asked for a steak. "How's the embroidery coming along?" he asked. It was one of his talking points from his note cards.

"I got two new orders this week. The women give me a basic idea of what they want, and they let me develop a design of my own. I like being creative."

"Still just women from the Relief Society?"

"You have to start somewhere."

"I just don't want your source to die off."

"I'll worry about that when I get there."

It was only a casual remark, but it struck Rick as terribly foolish. People never planned ahead, never looked at the bigger picture. That was the reason the country was in the mess it was. Everyone could see that sub prime mortgage rates were bad news waiting to happen, but everyone wanted to put off doing something about it till they were forced to, and by then, it was too late. Deregulation on Wall Street was bound to bring trouble, but no one wanted to worry till they had to, and by that point, disaster was unavoidable. Even the Church was moving more in this direction. When Rick was a boy, they were commanded to have a two-years' supply of everything, in case of disaster. Now they were only asked to have a few months' worth of food. But at least there was still some small sense of preparing for the future, he supposed.

And yet there was no conception that Mormons needed to press for efforts to control climate change. Mormons were almost exclusively Republican and as such felt almost universally that businesses should be free to do whatever they wanted. Being successful at business meant having a good, upright character, regardless of any damage to the environment your company created. Even if Christ did come back and usher in the Millennium, that Millennium was going to take place on the Earth. Didn't the Church want the planet to be a place where a Utopia was possible?

Rick knew he was extrapolating too far from the point. Embroidery on a sewing machine was just Nancy's pastime to make a few extra bucks and feel useful, but still, this nonchalance was an attitude Rick didn't like. He'd suggested to Ted that he start studying Spanish as soon as he received his call, but the boy kept putting it off, playing computer games with his friends when he wasn't listening to music, as if the inevitable were not just around the corner.

"Do you have any favorite colors you're working with now?" asked Rick.

"I like green as a base color, but I like to liven it up with reds and yellows and purples."

"Any stitch in particular you're having fun with?"

Nancy looked at him coldly. "You know perfectly well you couldn't care less about any of this."

How could a guy build up a rapport with his wife when she could see right through him? It was like decorating a deciduous tree for Christmas. Rick decided it was time to move on to another talking point. "What's your next lesson for the Laurels?"

"Hope chests," Nancy said promptly.

Rick laughed, hoping his obvious nonchalance would soften Nancy. "Sorry," he said. "You can't even get our own girls interested. You think you'll have any more luck with the other teenagers?"

"Those girls look up to me, despite Shelly and Karen. It's awkward having a 16-year-old and a 17-year-old of my own in the class, but the girls don't undermine me."

"No hope chest rebellions?"

"I've already told them I'd kill them if they laughed or made fun during class."

"Good luck."

But Rick felt a little comforted after his earlier gloomy thoughts. Hope chests made girls think of the future, plan for the day they'd be married. It was a compartmentalized planning, but it was something, and didn't they all compartmentalize? Some people planted trees right next to the house, where they'd eventually damage the foundation. Yet those same people might have an IRA set up from the time they were 25.

Rick pumped Nancy for some stories from her class on Sundays, hoping to garner a few points. She seemed to focus most on the things Karen and Shelly did. Karen had talked about being a junior before worrying about college entrance requirements. That was in a lesson entitled "The Glory of God is Intelligence." Shelly had talked about the importance of babysitting jobs as a teenager, to prepare the girls for motherhood. That was in a lesson called "Motherhood—Stepping Stone to the Future." Shelly had added that it was necessary to have a whole houseful of children to make up for all those people in Third World countries overpopulating. "We have to keep up the percentage of Mormons in the world," Nancy quoted their daughter as saying. "We need to propagate the Mormon species." Nancy laughed at the girl's cleverness.

Rick talked a little about work, and a little about the High Priests group at church, but as much as Nancy said she wanted Rick to open up, he had realized long ago she really just wanted him to listen. So he brought up another talking point during dessert—Sister Riley, the Relief Society president. "Any new horror stories?"

Nancy sighed deeply and put her fork down. "That woman," she said.

Rick gave what he hoped was a supportive glance.

"Do you know what she said to Marilyn today?"

"What?"

"She said Marilyn didn't have a kindergartner's skill at crafts." She picked up her fork again and pointed it at Rick. "*I* taught Marilyn everything she knows, so I could tell Barb was really making a dig at me."

"Maybe you shouldn't go to these luncheons."

"I need to grow my embroidery business. Sunday's not enough."

"But if it's just going to make you upset…"

"You watch the news every night," Nancy countered. "And that makes *you* upset."

She had a point there, Rick thought. Just yesterday, there had been a report about the failure of a pollution control bill in the Senate. This came a day after a report detailing the extinction of 30,000 species a year around the world. The planet had experienced five major extinction events in its history. The most famous was that which occurred 65 million years ago and killed off the dinosaurs. But even that event only involved the extinction of 75% of the world's species. The one at the end of the Permian killed off a whopping 95% of all species. Scientists were saying that the world was currently in the middle of a sixth extinction event. What was different about this one was that it wasn't caused by a comet impact or eruption of a supervolcano. This one was caused almost entirely by humans.

It was bad enough that average people were so thoughtless, but it downright infuriated Rick when he heard Mormons shrug off the disaster. "Oh, God will take care of it all during the Millennium." When Rick pointed out to Church members that God had made people stewards over the planet, they shrugged again and said, "We have the right to do what we want. And who cares if a few bugs or plants or birds go extinct? There are plenty more out there." If Rick pushed even further when encouraged by someone who offered a glimpse of intelligence, he might hear back, "If God has the ability to resurrect all of us people, why can't He just resurrect a few animals from each of the dead species, too? Then there will be no problem." When Rick saw what he was up against, he just started to feel very, very old.

Sometimes, Rick thought that the best thing that could happen to the planet was a pandemic bigger than the influenza outbreak that killed 20 million people in 1918, bigger even than the Black Death which killed a third of Europe in the Middle Ages. Perhaps Nature would strike back and kill off two or three billion people by allowing a virus to mutate. Perhaps humans would be evil and stupid enough to engage in biological warfare and kill off so many people that the rest of the planet could recover from their presence. Rick felt guilty about the fact that he never donated to medical charities or research. But sometimes he *wanted* people to die. Except for his tithing, Rick gave exclusively to conservation organizations. He wanted the Earth to be a wonderful place for the select few who would inherit it during the Millennium.

"Can't you guys weed Barbara out of the presidency?" Rick asked. "You all hate her."

"She's like those horsetails you love and I hate," said Nancy, referring to the plant Rick insisted on growing in the back yard along the fence. Its history went back to the age of the dinosaurs. It was one of the species that didn't die off then, like the gingko tree, and Rick felt they deserved to be propagated so they would last 100 million more years.

"You mean she's old?" Rick asked sarcastically.

"She has a prominent genealogy. No one dares touch her."

This comment made Rick feel irritated again. His own Church background only went back three generations, and he sometimes resented the attitude of people whose line went back to Brigham Young or Joseph Smith's time. These people treated new converts like simple-minded cretins. He could see it in his own family, too. Nancy's family had converted when she was 16, and Rick's parents always acted as if Rick had married outside the faith.

He wondered why people respected a human line that went back maybe 150 or 200 years and yet had no sense of awe at all for a sequoia that alone had lived 1500 years already. Not its family, but that single individual tree itself. Not many tree species had such long-lived members, but even their rarity didn't produce any sense of wonder. The truth was that cutting down even regular fir trees and spruce and oak that were 100 years old seemed a horrible sin to Rick.

He wondered sometimes about vegetarians who wouldn't eat "meat" and yet had no trouble eating fish. If a cow had a right to life, why didn't a fish? At the same time, why was it okay to kill a living plant but not a chicken? If chickens were morally superior to potatoes, what was wrong with saying humans were equally superior to pigs? No matter how you looked at it, people only existed by killing other living things, at whatever level those other beings might exist.

So what was wrong with killing whales? Or a tree that was larger than even the biggest dinosaur?

Part of it was in fact the grandeur. Rick didn't feel particularly bad that polio and smallpox were driven to extinction. Of course, whether or not viruses were technically ever alive in the first place was debatable. Yet Rick didn't feel overly terrible when a rat was killed. But if a poison dart frog went extinct, it did seem a tragedy. Maybe the frog wasn't big, but it was certainly pretty, wasn't it? So was his desire to protect the environment solely an aesthetic concern, not a moral one?

"Rick?" asked Nancy.

"Yes, dear?"

"I asked what you thought about that."

Rick had of course lost the thread of the conversation and hoped to bluff. "I think you need to do what makes you happy and not worry about them."

Nancy stared at him. "Well, what would make me happy is to give those boys poison ivy, or feed them to Audrey in the Little Shop of Horrors. But I guess I can't do that."

Rick realized they were talking about the vandals again. "Do you want me to look for them tonight?"

"They probably won't be out till 3:00 in the morning. And they certainly won't be in our neighborhood again."

"Well, let's go to the park instead of seeing a movie. It'll do us good to be in nature for a while."

"I don't like nature. I like roses."

"Come on. We can make out on a park bench."

"Oh, please."

Rick nodded. All evening he'd been thinking about the withering away of his sexual relationship with Nancy. Romance had slowed down considerably after Ted arrived and had almost died off completely after the girls came. Rick and Nancy now had sex maybe five times a year. Nancy never seemed interested but would apparently acquiesce when she felt the desire to do a charitable deed. Rick wondered what an eternity of eternal marriage would be like with an eternity of eternal abstinence. What if you didn't even qualify for godhood in the first place if you didn't have a godly desire for sex? Gods had to like sex, didn't they, if they were having billions of spirit children throughout the eons?

From what Rick could tell from overhearing conversations with the other High Priests, sex was definitely on the decline

36

among most of the more righteous couples in the ward. If they didn't succeed at marriage, though, they wouldn't get to the Celestial Kingdom and become gods. Rick couldn't help but wonder if gods themselves could become extinct if they weren't able to create more gods to come after them. You could never really be extinct if you lived forever, but if you failed at creating happy and prosperous offspring, wasn't old age in and of itself pointless?

"Maybe we should just go home then." Some days, Rick simply felt he was dying a slow death.

"Whatever."

They drove home in silence, Rick wondering why his own procreation seemed so meaningless to him. He should at least feel proud about Ted's missionary work, but somehow even planting a few seeds of the gospel in the jungles of Central America didn't seem to make up for the multitude of worldly weeds that were going to sprout up all around them. Maybe it really was only in the Millennium that the world would be habitable for the good people left behind. Then again, if only good people were allowed on the planet during that period of peace, that might mean an entire world population of only twenty million people. That's probably what it would take for humans not to destroy the planet. It wasn't their goodness during the Millennium that counted so much as their low numbers.

When they got home, Rick found a message on the machine from his brother about the wake. He went out to sit on the front porch alone to relax, and he saw that the vandals had even killed the five oak seedlings he was growing from his own acorns. Every year, Rick grew several seedlings, and when they reached two or three feet, he would put an ad in the paper to sell them for $5 apiece. When he found a person who seemed legitimately concerned about reforestation, whether urban or rural, Rick would give all five trees away for free. It wasn't enough to donate to American Forests and the Nature Conservancy every year. He wanted to take part personally in helping the environment. Rick would have grown more oaks, but Nancy thought pots full of seedlings weren't pretty to look at. Rick thought they were beautiful.

Thinking about his grandfather, and his 80-year-old oak, and the pettiness of the world, Rick grew angrier and angrier. He *would* stay up all night and roam the neighborhood to see if he could find those vandals. It wasn't as if there was any point getting into bed with Nancy.

Rick knew the type who had done this. He remembered when he was a boy, maybe 11, he'd read in the newspaper about a study that showed plants had feelings. Scientists "murdered" some plants in the presence of others and measured the electrical activity in the "witness" plants. They showed an excitation during the assault on their fellow plants. Further, when other people came into the room later, there was no change in resting electrical activity, but when the "murderers" returned, the plants became more active again.

Rick had told a neighborhood boy about the study, but rather than becoming impressed, the boy gleefully reached over and broke a branch off a plant in Rick's front yard. Rick had yelled at him, and the boy had laughed. For years afterward, for *years*, every time the boy passed by, he would break a branch or strip some leaves or do something else that antagonized Rick.

Why were people so hateful?

How could his grandfather be getting sex at 101 when Rick couldn't get any at 45?

Why was the Relief Society president the bitchiest woman in the congregation?

Why were people still trying to kill 1200-year-old trees?

Why did he not love Nancy any more?

It was 10:45 by now, and Rick stretched and decided to take a walk to see just how widespread the destruction of the lawn killers was. Every single lawn on his block had clear damage. He turned the corner and saw that every lawn in the block behind him was damaged, too. These must be awfully rich kids, to afford all that herbicide simply for a few nights of fun. They wouldn't want to keep spending so much money just on a prank, though. It wasn't free like slashing tires. As awful as their work had been, Rick took some comfort in knowing it must be nearing its end.

On the next block, thank goodness, everything seemed normal. Out by the curb at one house, there was a five-foot tree limb which had been trimmed from some tree on the property. Rick didn't much approve of trimming, either, but it was a compromise he could live with. He noticed that the branch was just the right size and shape to make into a walking stick, and that somehow made its sacrifice a little more acceptable, so he picked it up.

To Rick's surprise, the branch was wet. It hadn't been raining, though, he thought, frowning. Had some dog peed on it? He lifted the stick and found that it had a chemical smell. It was herbicide. Rick looked at the branch in confusion. What kind of idiot would pour herbicide on something already dead? He couldn't help but think of the factories spilling chemicals into rivers every day, sending carcinogenic gases into the atmosphere. There were a lot of stupid people out there.

Rick walked up to the bushes on the property and inhaled. They were covered with the poison. He realized with a start that some herbicides could be absorbed through the skin and were quite dangerous. But he wasn't willing to put the heavy stick down. Those vandals must still be in the area. He'd find them and bash their car to pieces. That would teach them. He started trotting up the street.

Rick found them in the next block, pouring a container of liquid around the base of a 55-foot tree. There were two teenage boys, just as he figured. Rick wanted to castrate them so they couldn't pass on their evil, defective genes. They didn't notice him walk up. But they turned when they heard the sound of glass breaking.

"Shit!"

"Fuck!"

"What do you think you're doing, old man?"

"I'm breaking your windows."

There was a short laugh. "That's not our car."

Rick stopped. He hadn't counted on that. He heard a car door open several feet further up and saw a teenage girl step out. She was lovely, even in this light, and Rick found himself brushing his hair back. Then he noticed the two young men walking slowly toward him. They looked menacing, but the people inside the house had surely heard the glass, too, and would be looking outside.

"So you want to be a vigilante?"

"It's better than being a vandal."

There was another laugh. "We're not vandals. We're missionaries."

"What?"

"We even go door to door."

The girl had joined them by this point. She showed Rick her necklace, which had a five-pointed star on it, a pentagram. "The devil has power over this world," she said in a sultry tone. "People are already doing a pretty good job of ushering in the kingdom of Hell, but we wanted to bring Hell to the world a little faster."

Rick stepped backward. What an outrageous thing to say. Were they just trying to freak him out? Trying to scare him?

"You people have your organizations to preach about God," said one of the boys, "but we have organizations, too."

Rick remembered seeing a story on the news about self-proclaimed vampires. These young people became obsessed with the idea and literally drank each other's blood, or picked people up in bars and drank their blood. There was nothing supernatural about them. They were just crazy freaks. He wondered if he'd stumbled upon something similar.

"We have the NRA," the boy continued. "Drug cartels. The tobacco industry. Oil companies." He smiled. "The World Wrestling Federation. Lots of organizations."

Now they were just teasing him.

"And pesticide companies," the boy went on. "And Harrah's, and Blackwater, and lots, lots more."

These kids weren't vandals, Rick realized. They were True Believers. He recognized the zeal in their voices. Rick wondered if maybe there were more people dedicated to doing bad things in this world than good things. He stepped back further and felt grass under his feet. There certainly was no

Satanic impulse behind all those groups, however unpleasant they might be. But if these kids believed it, they really might be fanatical enough to spend all their Burger King wages on herbicide, the way Mormon kids saved for their missions. Even Ted had saved a little. Too bad Ted didn't have the commitment these kids had.

"But if we go to jail, we won't be able to continue our work."

The boys were only a few feet away now. Rick waved his branch in the air to stop their advancement. The teen on the right made a quick motion, and Rick felt a heavy stone hit him on the side of the head. The blow dazed him, and the break in his concentration was all the group needed. They were on him in an instant.

The two boys pinned Rick down while the girl forced his mouth open and poured in some weed killer. Rick didn't mean to swallow, but it was instinctive, and they kept pouring and pouring. Swallowing seemed the only way to avoid drowning. He almost wished he *would* drown. But if he were going to be killed, it was a shame it hadn't been back before he had kids, before he'd contributed to a bigger carbon footprint. It was like Arlo Guthrie having kids before he realized he had a genetic disease that would kill both him and his kids. Rick should have died while he was young. If these teenagers kept dealing with this poison every night, though, they'd soon become toxic themselves. Maybe *they'd* die. That would be good. He started to pick himself up.

Then the boys were kicking him, in the legs, the arms, his chest, in the face. Rick didn't understand. These were just supposed to be bored kids out for some mischievous fun. What had humans evolved into?

Rick felt blood pouring from his cut lips, from his cheeks, onto the grass beneath him drenched in herbicide.

"Come on," said the girl. "It's too risky to stay around here. Let's head out to the apple orchards."

"He's still looking at us."

The girl picked up Rick's walking stick and raised it into the air slowly. She smiled at Rick and gave him a wink. Rick actually started to smile back. Then, as he thought about comets and supervolcanoes and pestilence and loggers, he watched as the girl brought the heavy stick down upon his head.

Betty's Dream Date

"I hope I'm still alive in the year 2000," said Betty. "I'm sure the Second Coming will happen by fifteen years from now. I want to be alive when the Millennium starts."

"Things might get bad first, though," said Alex, looking a little too worried as he said it, Betty thought. She was trying to focus on the positive.

She tickled Alex's foot with her own as they squatted in the swimming pool, to make him smile. "Yes, but wouldn't it be great not to die, just to change to a resurrected body in the twinkling of an eye?"

"Some of us might not be worthy of that," said Alex. "We might get zapped."

Betty looked at Alex in disbelief. He was always so insecure and needed constant ego stroking. "Oh, of course you're worthy," she said. "You're a stake missionary. You're Single Adult chair in the stake. You're second counselor in the elders quorum."

"Yeah, well..."

"Shari always said you were a perfect gentleman on your dates. You're still a virgin, aren't you?"

"So far."

Betty looked at Alex, who seemed depressed again. It was no wonder he felt bad. Betty's daughter Shari had broken up with him three years ago, halfway though his mission to the Netherlands. Betty had been so upset with Shari then for dumping what seemed to Betty like the perfect dream date. Sure, Shari had married another Mormon in the temple, so that was good, but Betty didn't like the new guy as much as she liked Alex.

A person never quite got over being second choice, Betty knew. And Alex hadn't seen his girlfriend in over a year now. It had to be hard on him.

Betty looked at Alex's face, glowing in the sunshine so that he gave off light even when he was down. He was so handsome and so righteous and… and… well, he was always so *nice* to Betty. When Shari dumped him, Betty had decided she would take over writing to Alex in Europe once a week for the rest of his mission. He needed her strength while he was out doing the Lord's work, and she would give it to him.

"You're a good man," Betty insisted. "You come visit me and George once a month. Not many 23-year-olds spend their Saturdays with people in their sixties."

"It's hardly a chore."

"You won't get zapped. If *I* know you're special, and God knows more than me, then *He* knows you're special, too. All we have to do is endure to the end."

Betty rubbed her foot up against Alex's calf. They were playing in the above ground swimming pool George set up every year to help them through the sweltering summers here in Slidell in southeast Louisiana. George set it up on their one-acre property between the mobile home and the cabinet shop he'd built across the yard. They didn't have air conditioning, so Betty and George took several dips throughout the day, every day. It kept them young, too, to play with each other all the time.

And it was only natural that she liked to play with Alex, too. They were such good friends.

"How's Anne?" Betty asked. It was always easy to remember the name of Alex's fiancée' in Amsterdam. It was the same as Anne Frank's name. Betty had given Alex a copy of the diary one year for Christmas. She liked to give him gifts that showed she'd put some thought into them. A diary written in Amsterdam where Alex had served showed she was trying to please him.

On other occasions, Betty had given him the book *Hans Brinker* and another book with photographs of Amsterdam. She'd also given him a Church book called *Faith Promoting Stories* and another called *Stories from the Kingdom*, both filled with true stories of how wonderful life could be when you chose to live the right way as he was doing. He always seemed slightly worried when he was with her, and she was afraid he might be having doubts. She never had any doubts, though, and she was sure the Lord had big plans for him. He'd be a stake president, certainly. Probably even a Regional Rep. And maybe even more. It was exciting being in the company of such goodness.

Betty had also given Alex a poem she'd written for him, and once she picked up a volcanic rock at a garage sale, since Alex was studying geology at the University of New Orleans.

And for his birthday last month, she'd given him a Speedo swimsuit, to show she recognized his efforts to lose 25 pounds over the past year. He probably only weighed about 140 now and looked pretty good. He'd never looked bad, of course. She knew the suit was a little immodest, but she wanted him to feel good about his body. She was glad he was wearing it now. It showed she was really helping his self-esteem. It proved she was useful.

"Anne's fine." Alex swam away from Betty to the other side of the pool. Betty followed him.

"Any idea when you might get married?"

"Not till I graduate, at least."

"Then I've got you for another year." She giggled and tickled his thigh playfully.

"We may never get married, Betty." Alex looked depressed again.

"She doesn't want to come to America? Did y'all have a fight?"

Alex swam away to the other side of the pool again, and Betty followed this time as well.

"I may not be worthy, Betty."

Betty stared. "Why, that's impossible," she said flatly. "You're the most righteous person I know. You're such an example for me. I thank God every day for letting me know you." She put her hand on his arm underneath the water.

Alex looked at her and then looked away. "I—I have strong sexual urges," he said softly.

Betty laughed. "Is that all?" she said, squeezing his arm. "George always had strong sexual urges, too. Still does. Some people just feel it more than others. It's not a sin."

"But if you act on it…"

"Have you?" Betty looked closely at Alex, but he turned away.

"No," he mumbled.

"Even if you have, it's not the end of the world." She hesitated a moment and then moved closer to Alex so that her body was touching his. "I've never told anyone this before, not even my own kids, but George and I…when he was going off to Korea…well, anyway, we weren't virgins when we got married after he came back, but we'd repented by then and were still able to have a temple wedding."

Alex looked at her strangely. He wasn't judging her, was he? Betty couldn't bear it if he did. But Alex was too sweet to do a thing like that.

"And David," she went on, mentioning her son, "he's been disfellowshipped twice for having sex with his girlfriend, but she won't agree to marry him, and you can't expect a normal, healthy man to withstand all those hormones forever. It's all perfectly natural." She giggled again. "*I* don't bother you, do I, when I hold your hand when we go on walks?" She pinched his arm playfully.

"It doesn't seem fair," said Alex, "that you guys can have sex and it's all okay. But I've been fighting hard all these years to stay a virgin, and all you have to do is say you're sorry and everything's fine. You're even on a higher level than I am, because I still think about it all the time."

"Oh, thinking about it isn't a sin." Betty laughed. "Or we'd all be in trouble."

Betty looked up then and saw George approaching in his trunks from the cabinet shop. George always had to come out when he heard Betty and Alex get in the pool. Betty couldn't tell if he was jealous that Alex was alone with her, or just jealous that they were having fun while he was working. She swam across the pool to greet him as he climbed into the water. Once he was in, he glided back and forth across the pool a couple of times and then stopped near Alex. Betty came over and sat on George's knees.

"Alex needs you to talk to him about your strong sex drive," Betty said simply. "He's worried about his."

Betty saw Alex's face turn pink, and she thought it was adorable that he was so shy.

"I need to have sex at least three or four times a week," he said matter-of-factly, looking right at Alex without embarrassment. He almost seemed to be boasting, Betty thought. Men were so weird about sex. "I could actually have it every day," he went on, "but I have to take Betty's feelings into account."

"So he masturbates on days when I'm not in the mood."

Alex's face turned even brighter pink, and Betty giggled again. It was kind of fun talking about all this so frankly. They were so close there was no reason not to. She'd often been tempted to discuss sex with Alex, and now she wondered why she'd waited this long.

"But he always makes me watch," she said.

"It's not a sin if you're still doing it as a couple."

"I know you must masturbate," said Betty, feeling even closer to Alex by saying it. "It's only natural. We caught David five or six times before he moved out. But that's a minor sin. Nothing to worry about."

Betty saw Alex look at George and then blush again. A cloud moved away from the sun, and Alex looked up into the sky a moment and then ducked his head under the water. Betty giggled. It was so sweet that he was this embarrassed about the subject. When he resurfaced, he stole another look at George.

"I could use a fruit drink," George announced. When he stood up and started climbing the ladder out of the pool, Betty could see he had an erection from all the sex talk. She noticed that Alex had seen it, too, and she giggled again.

Alex let her climb out of the pool before him, and when she turned around to watch him get out of the pool, he kept his front turned away from her, and then he wrapped a towel around himself immediately. Betty smiled, knowing why.

Betty went inside and cut up some bananas and peaches and put them in a blender with some ice and then chopped it all up. She poured out the content into two glasses and handed one glass to George and another to Alex.

"How interesting," said Alex, sipping his.

"What?"

"You put pepper in it."

Betty frowned and took the glass back. She saw lots of tiny black specks. How odd. Then she noticed one of the specks was a little clawed foot. She'd chopped up a roach. She was mortified and emptied the drink into the sink. She felt contaminated and filthy.

It was the same horrible feeling she'd experienced last night at the Bishop's storehouse when she was picking up her free food from the Church. She was lifting her first bag of groceries out of a cart when she saw Alex, who was volunteering that night, filling food orders for poor members of the Church. She'd never told Alex that she and George got food every month from the Bishop's storehouse, but now he knew they were on Church welfare. It seemed too private a thing to share with him. It wasn't a sin to be poor, but sometimes she felt it was.

Betty washed out the blender and made a new batch of drinks. Alex and George were laughing, but Betty still felt terrible. George worked so hard all day. It was her job to be a good homemaker, and she had to do it well. And Alex was just so sweet, she hated to have him realize her failings. It made her feel she was living a lie.

"How about a game of Six Across?" said George.

"You have time?" asked Betty.

"I need a break, too. You get to hog Alex all to yourself the whole day. I want a little of him, too." He laughed.

Betty was happy that George seemed to like Alex as much as she did. He never complained when she used their most expensive foods on him when he came, a roast with carrots and potatoes, Alex's favorite dish. She also always prepared a cheesecake, the only time during the month she made a dessert, given her increasingly worsening diabetes. She'd had to switch from pills to insulin injections six months ago. "I guess I'm just too sweet," she joked.

Sometimes, though, George acted a little petulant that Betty talked about Alex so much. She simply wanted to share her happiness with the person who mattered most, of course, her husband. But on the nights after Alex had spent the day in Slidell, Betty knew she always had to go the extra mile in bed with George. He seemed so aggressive on those evenings. She couldn't tell if he was mad at her or mad at Alex or what, but Betty always had to make sure George understood that Alex was just a friend, that the man she really wanted was him.

Betty watched now as George pulled out the large, circular wooden board he'd drilled depressions in. The design was a six-pointed star, so six players could participate, helpful when the whole family was there. The game was basically a cross between Sorry and Parcheesi with a couple of twists thrown in, played with marbles. George had invented it himself, and Betty loved playing with both Alex and George. She used to let Alex win, till George one day told her, "Alex is a big boy. Be his friend, not his mother."

As they were sitting at the table in their swim suits playing, Betty's Siamese cat jumped up and began walking across the board. "This is no time for a pussy," said George, but as he reached for the cat, it sneezed.

Betty hated when George talked like that, making sexual jokes. It was so unseemly. "She's allergic to people hair," said Betty, laughing at her own, clean joke. Talking frankly about sex as they'd done earlier was one thing. That somehow seemed pure and good. But joking about it always struck Betty as tawdry.

Yet maybe George was right. Alex seemed so worried about sex that maybe they did need to get him to lighten up a little. "This pussy's always here when you want her," said Betty, lifting the cat off the table and setting her down on the floor. "And even when you don't want her." She laughed, unsure if what she said was actually funny or not.

Betty was sitting next to Alex, her bare foot resting on his, while George sat on the other side of the counter. She almost missed her turn once because she was admiring the way Alex's goatee reflected the light. She caught George looking at her, and she wanted to hit herself. Alex was a special friend, and she'd told George that over and over. Sometimes, he seemed to be happy about it, and other times he seemed upset. She was sure he knew all they did was talk. They talked about Betty's children, and about the gospel, and about life. They were almost like girlfriends, Betty assured George. It just happened that he was a handsome young man instead. But that didn't change their relationship.

"Your turn, sweetie," said George, smiling.

They played for about 45 minutes, and then George went back out to the cabinet shop to work again on the cabinets he was building for the bishop's new house.

Betty and Alex went to sit on the divan, the cat rubbing up against Betty's right leg, and her left leg pressed up against Alex. They talked about the latest temples that had been announced recently, and how exciting it was to be living in the last days.

"Of course, the world is so perverse now," said Betty. "It used to be innocent in the old days. It was like living in Archie comics."

"Well, it's not innocent any more," said Alex, looking depressed again. Just as he said it, Betty noticed the sun being blotted out by sudden cloudcover. The shadow on his face made her remember something.

"Of course," she said slowly, "I recall my mother telling me once she was raped when she was ten, and that must have been back in the early part of the century. And I remember having a slumber party when I was 13, and my girlfriend wanted to French kiss me. She said it was so we'd be more practiced when it came time to kiss boys. But now I wonder. I didn't think anything of it at the time. I mean, I said no, of course, but it wasn't till all this talk of homosexuality started in these last few years that I remembered that." She shook herself as if to knock off the memory. "Anyway, *we* have a pure relationship, and that makes me stronger spiritually." She giggled. "So I always feel I'm in your debt."

"You shouldn't put me on a pedestal like that. I'm as human as anyone else."

"Yes, but you're a *good* human."

"Betty—"

Just then, the phone rang, and Betty hurried over to answer it.

"Oh, hi, Shari!" said Betty brightly. "Guess who's here? Alex!"

But then Betty heard the tone in Shari's voice, and she grew concerned. Shari lived in Alabama, in Montgomery. She hoped there wasn't any trouble. Montgomery was too far away for Betty to be of much help.

"Paul and I are getting a divorce," said Shari abruptly. "He's having an affair with the babysitter. Can you believe that?"

"Oh, my god." The world really was perverse.

"He says he's taking both the kids," said Shari without emotion. "But I get to keep the two cats, so I'm happy."

Betty could hardly believe what she was hearing. She knew Shari had never taken to motherhood the way she had, that she'd always been a little unnatural, but to be so cavalier about losing her children. The world must surely be coming to an end soon. How much longer could it be before Christ came back?

"Are you okay?"

"Yes, Paul says he already found me a little apartment. He's thought of everything apparently. I move out next week and start looking for a job right away."

"Do you want to move back home?"

"No. I don't think that would be a good idea."

Betty heard a crack of thunder and jumped. "Oh, it's about to storm here, Shari. I'd better get off the phone."

"You don't know the half of the storm that's coming."

"You watched the news?"

"Forget it, Mom."

Betty hung up, puzzled and upset. She went to sit back next to Alex, holding his hand in her lap. There was another crack of thunder and Betty tightened her grip on Alex's hand. She told him all about the conversation she'd just had, and she couldn't help but add, "I'm so glad you didn't marry Shari. You and I wouldn't have become such good friends. I like having you all to myself. I don't want to share you with anyone." She giggled, despite all the bad news she'd just heard. "I guess I'll have to make room for Anne, though, won't I?"

"I suppose."

"And of course, I don't mind sharing you with George."

"I like George."

"You know," said Betty, turning and looking straight into Alex's eyes, "it's funny talking to you about my kids since they're your age. But you don't seem 23. You seem like an equal." Then she raised her hand to her mouth quickly. "Of course, you're so much better than I am. And so much more mature, even at your age. I should be talking about trying to be *your* equal."

"I can assure you I wasn't offended."

It started raining outside, and they could hear the heavy drops hitting the roof. Betty went to check the crock pot and start finishing the rest of the dinner. She pulled a can of corn from the special pantry rack George had constructed. The rows slanted forward and had a little rail to keep the cans from falling onto the floor. But the rows could be added to from the rear, putting the cans in sideways, so the oldest can was always rolled to the front, with the newer ones behind. This kept the food rotating.

George had designed the pantry to keep their food storage fresh. They couldn't afford a year's supply like the Church said, but they were prepared as much as they could be at least with the proper tools. It was so nice being married to a man who listened to the Church leaders. If only God hadn't decided to test them so much with poverty. They could be leaders in the Church if they weren't so poor. George would be just right as a bishop or a stake High Councillor, and she'd be good as Relief Society president. They might even be able to serve as a mission president and his wife, but they'd never be in a position to afford supporting themselves for three years without pay.

Betty wished she could do something to let her goodness show. All she could really do was be good to Alex. He was struggling, and she could help him. It was as if God had given her both a service project *and* a friend in one. And she volunteered as the substitute organist at church, and she was one of the few women in her ward who always did her Visiting Teaching each month. It wasn't much, but Betty suspected that somewhere down the line, God had something special for her in mind. She could feel it.

It certainly helped that Betty had someone as special as Alex to help her be strong. She felt a tingling every time they were together. She knew it was the Holy Ghost simply witnessing to goodness in general. She sent up an extra little prayer of thanksgiving for that now and then continued with her dinner preparations.

Betty had a good meal prepared tonight, and she knew it. George came in around 6:30, wet from the rain, but he was still in his swim trunks, so it didn't matter. She could tell George disapproved of the Speedo she'd bought for Alex by the way he kept looking at them and frowning. But he was too nice to ever criticize anything she did for Alex. Even when she'd bought an expensive Dutch dictionary and grammar book so she could learn a little basic Dutch to impress Alex, he hadn't complained, despite their tight finances. "Whatever makes you happy," was all George would say. When she had learned to say "I love you" in Dutch to please Alex, George had insisted on learning the phrase, too, so he could say it to her as well.

George dried off and sat at the table, ready for dinner. Betty had just served the roast, carrots, potatoes, and corn when suddenly there was another loud clap of thunder and the lights went out.

"Oh, dear!" said Betty, grabbing Alex's shoulder.

It was still daylight but was almost black from the clouds. Betty fumbled around for some candles and soon had them lit.

"A candlelight dinner!" she said, giggling. "How fun! It's so romantic!"

But Betty saw the way George looked at her, staring deep into her eyes and then looking down at the table. Had she hurt his feelings? It wasn't as if she and Alex were on a date, after all. She'd have to be extra attentive to George this evening after Alex left.

She sat back down and soon things returned to normal. They all chatted and joked during the dinner, even after the few serious minutes when Betty had to tell George about Shari's call. "She wasn't cut out for traditional marriage, anyway," said George, shrugging. "Not everyone is." He looked down at the table again, so Betty knew he was still troubled about the call.

At the end of the meal, Betty brought out the cheesecake, cutting herself a small piece as well. She only cheated with Alex, and a little cheating now and then never hurt anyone. She would just increase her insulin a little later. Alex was worth breaking the rules a tiny bit every once in a while.

"You know the way to a man's heart, Betty," said Alex, grinning, and Betty giggled.

Just then the phone rang, and thinking it might be Shari again, Betty hurried to answer it. But it was the bishop.

"Sister Newton, I'm afraid I'm going to have to ask you to come in for an interview tomorrow."

Betty frowned. "Well, sure, but why?" Was she about to be called to an important position? It was about time.

"I don't quite know how to say this, but, well, your daughter called and told me you were having an affair with a young man named Alex from another stake. She said she's witnessed enough affairs to know one when she sees one. So you'll need to come in to tell me your side of all this."

Betty felt as if she'd been punched. Had Shari really accused her of infidelity? How could she have said such a thing? Betty's relationship with Alex was a pure thing, a good thing, and Shari was trying to make it ugly. What a horrid thing to do.

"Certainly, Bishop. We can meet tomorrow after Sacrament meeting."

She hung up the phone in a daze. She looked over at George and Alex, but she couldn't quite meet their eyes. She felt terribly betrayed, but then Alex put his hand on her arm, and suddenly, somehow none of it mattered any more. She laughed.

"What's wrong?" asked George.

"The bishop thinks Alex and I are having an affair. Shari told him."

Alex quickly removed his hand, and then George laughed and laughed. Alex began laughing, too, and soon all three of them were howling.

"I—I hope you're not going to tell the bishop tomorrow that you had a candlelit dinner with Alex tonight."

"Oh, it's preposterous." Betty stood up and started clearing away the dishes.

George and Alex moved over to the divan, and when Betty finished, she joined them. "Move over, George. I want to sit between you." George didn't move over very far, though, so Betty had to squeeze to fit onto the sofa, her legs rubbing up against each of them. She grabbed Alex's hand and put it in her lap, and she took George's hand and put it in her lap, too.

"I'm not going to let the filthiness of the world change anything. *We* know we're pure. That's all that matters."

George talked for a while of a problem he was having designing one of the corner cabinets for the bishop and how he'd finally figured out a solution. Alex told them about a tricky principle he'd been having trouble with in geology, and the pneumonic device he'd developed to learn it better. Betty announced her latest phrase in Dutch, which she'd been waiting all day to say. "Ik ben zo blij u een deel van mijn leven bent." She was quite proud of herself.

Alex laughed. "I'm glad to be a part of y'all's life, too."

Alex normally liked to leave around 8:00, but it was still storming and the electricity was still out.

"You may have to stay all night," said Betty, squeezing Alex's hand. "The stoplights won't be working, either. It'll be a mess."

George laughed. "The bishop won't like that."

"Who cares what the bishop thinks!" Betty snapped. Then she looked at Alex and George and giggled again.

They stayed up talking about their favorite Book of Mormon stories till 10:00. It was still nasty out. When Betty yawned three times in a row, George said, "I think it's time for bed."

"I'll change the sheets in the spare bedroom." Betty stood up, stretching.

"No, let's have Alex sleep with us."

Betty turned to stare at George.

"I just think it'll be fun to have you explain to the bishop that yes, you 'slept' with Alex." He chuckled. Betty continued to look at him, and he added, "Don't worry, dear. I'll be there to protect you from his advances."

Alex put his face in his hands, and seeing that charming innocence again, Betty couldn't help but laugh. "You guys."

She felt strangely excited about sleeping with Alex for the first time. She wished Alex would sleep between them. There was an intimacy that even slumber parties could bring that was nice. But of course she knew George would sleep in the middle. That was okay, though. Just to know she was in bed with Alex would be kind of satisfying.

Betty wondered for a moment if maybe she *was* having a kind of affair with Alex.

But just because you loved someone didn't mean you wanted an affair. There were different kinds of love, weren't there?

Even though they'd been in their swim suits all day, when Betty saw Alex in his garments, she felt a little uncomfortable. Looking at him in his Mormon underwear, even though they came down to his knees, seemed somehow more revealing than the Speedo.

The three were all getting ready for bed by flashlight. They were in the addition now. Years ago, George had built a large bedroom onto the side rear of the mobile home. He said he wanted more space in bed. He wanted a king size water bed. And that would never fit in the existing bedroom, so he simply built a new room. He was planning to build another large room on the other side of the trailer, in the middle, to use as a living room. He did all the work himself, so it was just a matter of buying the materials. In their present condition, though, that was still asking a lot, Betty reflected. Being industrious was a gospel principle, but how could you live the gospel fully when you were too poor even to pay a full tithing?

Maybe George should charge the bishop more for his cabinets, Betty thought, if the man was going to accuse her of an affair.

Betty climbed into bed first, and she felt a little thrill when she saw George motion for Alex to get in next. Then George crawled in last and switched off the flashlight.

"Goodnight, everyone," said Alex.

Betty felt Alex's foot on hers, and she couldn't relax enough to fall asleep. Had she been worrying about the wrong thing all this time? Maybe it was Alex who wanted an affair with *her*. She suppressed a giggle and instead just smiled in the darkness. What a dear, innocent, charming boy. She knew Alex could never be attracted to her physically, of course. He was just attracted by her goodness. They brought out the best in each other. That was all this was about. She was so tired, but she didn't want the day to end just yet.

Betty let her hand move over so that she was just barely touching Alex's hand.

Then slowly, slowly, she emptied her mind and finally drifted wearily off to sleep.

There was blackness and silence for the longest time. Even the sound of the rain on the roof and the occasional thunder didn't disturb Betty. But eventually, she started dreaming. She could feel waves and hear the wind blowing. She was in a hurricane.

She jerked awake, and it took her a minute to realize where she was. The porch light wasn't on, and the room was black. But she could still hear the wind and feel the waves.

"George, what's going on?" She reached over, forgetting that Alex was next to her in the bed.

She couldn't quite tell what she was feeling. That was George's butt, wasn't it? But why was he thrashing around? Was he sick? Was he having a nightmare?

Betty suddenly felt a hand groping for hers. She could feel George's calluses. He was tugging at her. He needed help. She moved over, ready to assist him.

Right next to the thrashing body, Betty suddenly remembered that Alex was supposed to be in the bed, too. But where was he? Was George hurting him? Was George really that jealous after all? What was she going to do?

She reached over and in the darkness could feel George on top of Alex. She tried to pull them apart before Alex got hurt. What was George thinking? She still felt in a daze.

"No, no, sweetie. Just hold my hand. It's not a sin if we do it as a couple."

A hand grasped hers, and another hand fumbled around awkwardly for her breast. Betty was too dumbfounded to move.

The thrashing finally stopped as Betty heard George's deep sigh. Then she heard George whisper, "Ik houd van u." She couldn't believe what had just happened. But before she could think it through, George climbed on top of her, too, and she felt him prying open her garments.

Soon he was inside her, and she had to let him. He was her husband, and he needed her. Betty had always felt a little powerful in knowing that George couldn't get enough of her. But now? What was she to think?

It took her a moment to realize that it wasn't George inside of her. She squealed a little in terror.

"Yeah," whispered Alex. "Yeah."

She reached up and wrapped her arms around Alex's back. Then a callused hand grasped one of hers and held it.

"It's only an affair if just one of us is doing it," George whispered.

Betty couldn't remember feeling this way in a very long time. But was she going to hell?

No. George was right. This wasn't an affair. It was love. There was a difference.

Lightning flashed outside, and in that brief second of light, Betty could see Alex's face above her, grimacing in pleasure. Pleasure *she* was giving him. With her free hand, she pulled his face to hers and began kissing him.

A loud, low rumbling shook the trailer just as Betty felt her own body trembling. Alex collapsed on top of her a moment later. She held him for a moment, and then he rolled off between her and George.

Betty smiled and pressed up close to Alex, pushing him up against George. She put her hand on Alex's penis, feeling it now through his garments. She caressed it lovingly.

"Uh, Betty." There was a pause. "Betty." Another pause. "Betty!"

Betty jerked awake. There was dim light filtering into the bedroom from the kitchen, where the lights had come back on. It took Betty a moment to wake up.

George was awake by now, too, and looked over to see what was happening.

"You weren't thinking of having an affair just to spite Shari, were you?" asked George, smiling a little sadly.

Betty looked at George's face. He didn't look mad, but he looked perhaps a little disappointed, perhaps a little something else. Betty couldn't quite read his expression. She suddenly realized what she was doing with her hand, though, and let go with a start.

"I—I was dreaming," she stammered.

"Apparently."

"The storm is over and the electricity is back on. Maybe I should go."

Betty lay there quietly as Alex crawled out of the bed, got dressed, and headed out without speaking. George went out to the kitchen and turned off the light. But a dim beam still came through the window from the porch light outside.

"I'm sorry," Betty mumbled when George got back into bed.

He didn't say anything, but he climbed on top of her and forced his way inside roughly. Before long, he was pumping away vigorously. He kept at it for several minutes, much longer than usual, Betty thought, but he never did seem to finish. Betty could hardly endure it any longer.

Finally, George pulled out and lay beside her, still not having finished. Betty could hear him crying.

She held his hand, feeling his calluses, and then she softly began to cry as well.

The Bonds of Hell

"Mom, where am I supposed to stand? Where am I supposed to sit? Where am I supposed to kneel? What am I supposed to say? My stomach is all tied in knots."

"Susan," said Martha, "the temple worker will guide you. You don't need to worry about anything."

"I'm so nervous. I want my wedding to go perfectly."

"It will. You're being sealed to the man of your dreams."

Martha smiled at her daughter, and they talked for another twenty minutes about the reception. The wedding itself was pretty straightforward. There were no flowers or organist or soloist or anything else for a Mormon wedding. At least, not for a temple wedding. You just went to the temple, and the woman got her endowments. The man already had his because he'd gone on a mission. Then you went to the sealing room and knelt across the altar. You looked in the mirrors hanging on opposite walls, tilted just slightly so that the reflection of each mirror in the other angled off into infinity, to show the new couple what eternity was like. And then you were married. You'd be together forever, and your children would be yours forever, too.

Susan would still be Martha's, even after she married Cliff.

"Getting married is hell," said Susan.

"No, it's the doorway to heaven," said Martha, smiling.

Martha remembered her own wedding so many years earlier. It seemed like just yesterday. Well, no, it really seemed like three or four years ago, but it certainly didn't feel like more than two decades had passed. She'd met Don at a Single Adults dance, and he'd stepped on her feet twice and spit a piece of potato chip onto her dress once when he laughed during a break in the music.

But he'd kept her laughing and dancing all evening, and though the other girls rolled their eyes, Martha said yes when Don asked her out for the following weekend. It was the start of her biggest adventure, creating an eternal family of her own.

Martha gave Susan a kiss goodbye as the girl took off for her apartment. Susan still lived by the University of Utah, even though she'd graduated four months ago. Martha hoped her daughter would be more fertile than she had been. Martha had only been able to become pregnant twice, and she'd miscarried the other child. She'd never forget that awful day. Susan was almost two and had been crying all day from an ear infection. Martha was so tired, trying to take care of two children. She figured the one in her belly could take a back seat for just one day, and she picked Susan up every time the girl cried, which was about every fifteen minutes.

Martha was so afraid Susan would lose her hearing or that the infection would spread and become life-threatening. She couldn't imagine life without that precious little girl.

But then suddenly, when Susan twisted one time as Martha was picking her up, Martha felt something snap inside of her. Soon she was having cramps, and she had to call Don to hurry home from the office. She'd started bleeding before he made it through the front door. And Martha had just stood there crying and crying.

The doctor said later it had been a boy.

So Susan was all Martha had now in order to produce a lineage. She didn't really understand it. Her mother had had six children, and all of Martha's brothers and sisters had all had from three to seven children each. Why had she been stuck with the aberrant gene?

Well, Martha loved her siblings and didn't begrudge them their good fortune. She just hoped that now Susan would be able to bring her a houseful of grandchildren. She walked over to her bookcase and picked out a few of her old photo albums. Most people just had all their photos in chronological order. Martha had one album solely for couples—her parents, herself with Don, all her brothers and sisters with their spouses, her cousins and aunts and uncles and grandparents with theirs. It was an album exclusively for couples on their way to godhood. Then she had another album that was only family portraits, Celestial families in the making. She had a separate album for friends, and other albums for vacations or various miscellaneous events. Today, she looked at the couples and families.

This was what life was all about, making connections that would last throughout the ages. It was so wonderful to be Mormon and have the opportunity to develop eternal relationships. Other religions only allowed marriage "till death do you part." Martha didn't even understand how people like that could call their love real. They were getting into relationships with automatic divorces built right in. Why couldn't everyone see that the Mormon way of tying relatives together was better?

Martha prepared green bean casserole and ham for dinner, one of Don's favorite meals. It was such a happy time, she felt she should do something special.

"How was work today, dear?"

"Okay."

"Anything interesting happen?"

Don finished chewing a bite of ham. "Not really."

"Was Alex a pest again today?"

"Let's not talk about Alex."

They continued eating in silence. "Susan came over to talk about the wedding," said Martha a few minutes later. That ought to generate some discussion.

"I trust that all is going well?"

"Yes."

Hmm. How had he managed to circumvent the whole topic with one question? Well, maybe he was just tired again. He seemed exhausted so much lately. At least she'd made apple pie for dessert. Don loved apple pie, and he deserved some special attention after a long day away from her. Martha had learned to be understanding. It was part of what made their marriage work. Even gods would have lots on their mind. Being understanding was a Celestial skill she had cultivated.

She looked at her photo albums again after the dishes were done.

The following day, Martha had to run some errands. She saw a young man smoking outside the grocery while talking to his girlfriend, and she watched as a young woman wearing a sleeveless blouse carried a baby in a modern papoose inside Walgreens. So many people lived oblivious lives, committing sins just large enough to keep them from the Celestial Kingdom. The Word of Wisdom and chastity in dress were commandments whether you were a Mormon or not.

Martha wondered if she should say something to the young mother. She knew about the Golden Questions. Perhaps she could ask a variation. She went up to the young woman, touching her gently on her bare shoulder.

"Excuse me."

"Yes?"

"Do you love your baby?"

The young woman instinctively moved away. "Yes."

"Don't you want to be with your baby forever?"

"Of course I do." The woman moved another step away, and Martha moved over as well.

"You can have that if you live gospel principles."

"Uh, I've got to get home. I have to meet my Mom."

"Do you love your mother?"

The woman left her basket and hurried out of the store. Martha bit her lip. She hadn't handled that very well, but then, she'd never been a missionary, either. Still, trying to save families had to gain her a point or two. It was good to have bonus points in case you missed a couple of the other exam questions God gave you, like guessing what your daughter wanted when she turned sixteen, or being able to perform in bed even when you weren't in the mood.

Martha went home and called Susan, who didn't answer, and then she started working on dinner.

The next couple of days went well, and then Martha received a call from her sister, Dell. "What's up?" asked Martha cheerily. Dell was favorite sister, just a year younger than Martha. "How's Rob?" Dell's husband always seemed to catch the latest cold going around. He had bad knees and dandruff and rosacea and fingernail fungus. The kids in the family had always been scared of him, treating him like a leper, but Martha knew he could crack wicked jokes. He owned a small chain of stores and was a High Priest. And from a distance, he was actually attractive. Martha always felt that Dell had married well. Rob was going to be brilliant catch in the Millennium.

"I'm afraid I'm going to miss the wedding reception."

There was only enough room around the altar for immediate family. Usually, only parents and a handful of others attended any given temple wedding. The rest of the clan would have to settle for the reception, often held in the church gym.

"No, you can't," said Martha, laughing at what she was sure was a joke. "You promised to bring punch. Did you and Rob get a good deal on a trip to Hawaii or something?"

"I'll either be deathly ill on chemotherapy, or I'll actually be dead," said Dell calmly.

Martha was dumbstruck. Rob might make a sick joke like that, but Dell wouldn't. "What are you talking about?"

"I have ovarian cancer." She sighed. "I'm only 44. I was really hoping for one last baby to add to the family. Now it'll always be just the five kids."

Just five? Martha knew Dell didn't mean to be insulting. "You can have more in the Millennium," said Martha. "We can get pregnant together then."

"I suppose."

"And you'll help raise a dozen grandchildren before you go, so you'll have even more experience before you have any more kids of your own in the Millennium."

"Well, you better get tested, too. The doctor says there's a genetic component. I'll have to call Sally as well."

"Don't you worry about us. You concentrate on getting better."

Martha didn't want to talk about the possibility of death, but Dell did. Her cancer was advanced and there was only a slim chance that treatment would work. After half an hour of hearing medical details, Martha finally realized she was going to lose her favorite sister.

The news was devastating, and yet, her Mormonism came to the rescue again, as it had at every pivotal moment of her life. They were all sealed as a family. Once her parents had married in the Salt Lake temple fifty-five years ago, each child that came thereafter was automatically sealed to the family unit. And since all six siblings had each also married in the temple, all the new successive families were all still linked together forever as well. How did other people face losing a sister, without the benefit of the blessing Mormons had, knowing they'd be together again in the next world? The idea was just too depressing. It must be hell not to be Mormon. Even just losing Dell for a few years would be bad enough. How awful it would be to believe it was permanent.

Martha remembered a story she'd read in one of her Deseret books one day. A woman had been in a car accident and had temporarily died. On the other side, she was reunited with her mother, who'd died a few years previously. The mother told the woman not to give up on her brother, who'd been missing in action in Viet Nam for almost three years and was presumed dead. The woman recovered, and she told her sister-in-law not to remarry, that her brother was still alive. The sister-in-law waited, and a year later, the Viet Cong released the brother, and he was able to return home to his family. He said that about a year before his release, after a night of torture during which he was almost killed, he saw his mother and asked her to make sure his wife waited for him. The eternal bonds of the temple had allowed first the warning the sister received and then the reunion with the wife. How could anyone doubt the Church when they heard a story like that?

But the story also gave Martha pause. What *if* the sister-in-law had remarried? A woman, of course, was not allowed a second temple wedding, the way men were, so what would have happened if the woman had had several children with her second husband? Would they have been sealed to her anyway, and sealed to the first husband? Was the second husband just a sperm donor?

Well, in any event, God didn't let such an awkward situation arise. That's why he gave the woman the vision in the first place. The Lord gave the blessing of eternal family bonds, and he saw to it that they were in fact always a real blessing. Knowing she couldn't permanently lose Dell gave Martha some small degree of comfort now.

Martha and Dell decided they wouldn't tell the rest of the family about the treatment. "I don't want to take away from the wedding," said Dell. Her own children would have to know, but they'd be sworn to secrecy. Marriage was the key to propagating the family ties into the next generation, and it was essential that it be a happy occasion. Sally would be told to schedule a test only after the wedding was over. Martha appreciated that Dell was keeping an eternal perspective.

But a week later came even more distressing news. "Mom, Dad, Cliff and I have something important to tell you." Susan looked very nervous, and Martha was afraid they were choosing an exotic temple far away for the wedding, or perhaps even calling off the wedding altogether. What if it were something worse? Maybe Susan was already pregnant.

Of course, even pregnancy wouldn't be the end of the world. If they managed to have a temple wedding before the baby was born, the baby would still be sealed to them upon birth. And if the couple were disfellowshipped for the sex and had to wait a year to go to the temple, they could still have the baby sealed to them afterward, and at that point any future children would be automatically sealed, too. It was an extra step, but it wouldn't be an absolute catastrophe.

Unless they never made it back to the temple after missing their first chance. Some people who were married civilly never upgraded to a temple wedding. *That* would be unthinkable. That would be hell.

"What is it?" asked Martha cautiously.

Susan looked at Cliff, and he cleared his throat. "It's my Dad," he began uncomfortably. "I don't want to go into details, but... he's been excommunicated. He won't be able to go to the temple with us."

Martha and Don just looked at each other. "Did he choose to leave?" Martha asked carefully. "Will he be coming back after he repents?"

"I don't know if he'll be back," said Cliff. "I hope so." He paused. "But the immediate issue is the wedding."

"What do you mean?" asked Martha. "You're not calling it off? You're not postponing?" She looked anxiously at Susan. Martha wanted the marriage to be a done deal. Cliff was a returned missionary who had been an assistant to the mission president. He was elders quorum president now. He was good husband material. Martha wanted the grandchildren to start coming within a year.

"Mom," said Susan gently. "It's just that if Cliff's parents can't come to the wedding, we didn't think it would be fair to them to have you two there."

Martha looked at Don again. "But...but *we* didn't do anything wrong."

"It'll be a slap in the face if my Dad is the only one who can't come," said Cliff. "There will be 'weeping and wailing and gnashing of teeth.' You understand."

Martha most definitely did not understand. It *should* be a slap in the face for Cliff's father. If he became painfully aware that he alone was excluded from the wedding, he'd realize more acutely his position. He would not only be excluded from the temple but also from the Celestial Kingdom, which is what really mattered. He'd be kept away from his wife and children and grandchildren throughout eternity. That was the definition of hell, not the fact of merely being with Satan. *That* was Outer Darkness. Hell was being separated from God and your family. You were technically in hell even in a lower degree of heaven. Maybe being aware of it now would encourage Cliff's father to repent as he should. Pussyfooting around the issue would only be enabling him to continue living in sin. He'd be caught forever in the bonds of hell.

Then again, Martha wasn't quite sure she didn't want that for the man. He was keeping her from the wedding. How could she ever pretend to like Cliff's father after that? She was fortunate to like everyone in her own family, but she knew of people who had some horrendous brother or cousin or aunt. They might be good members of the Church on the surface, but the rest of the family had to hope that there was some catch that would keep these jerks out of the Celestial Kingdom so they wouldn't be stuck with them eon after eon.

Susan and Cliff left, and Don went to go work in the garage. Martha sat fuming in the kitchen. Why was all this happening to her? First Dell and now Cliff's father. Martha only had one daughter and she'd only be getting married one time. Why was God trying to ruin everything? He could have given Dell cancer a few months later, couldn't he? He could have had Cliff's father get caught sinning after the wedding, couldn't he? It wasn't fair.

Martha tried to relax and pray and meditate and read the scriptures, and finally she began to relax. The key point was that her daughter *was* getting married in the temple. That was all that really mattered, after all. And whatever problems Cliff's side of the family might have, *her* side was all still sealed and ready for the next life. Perhaps she shouldn't complain so much, Martha realized. She really still had it pretty good. Thank God for the Church. Even life itself would be endless torment without those sacred bonds it provided. Martha would still go to the temple, wait outside, and take pictures of the new couple outside that sacred building, for all posterity to see. She could still be a part of that special occasion. So she couldn't go inside. You made sacrifices for your family. That was what made the bonds stronger.

The following day, the invitations came in the mail. They were on thick ivory paper, textured, with a red wax seal. Inside was a lovely photo of Susan and Cliff, a copy of which Martha had already slipped into her "couples" album. There was also the date of the temple wedding, and an invitation to the reception. And Susan and Cliff had added something special. "In lieu of gifts, please consider donating a few dollars to the

Church welfare fund." They were so thoughtful. They'd surely make it to the Celestial Kingdom.

Then Martha had a terrible thought. What if they didn't *all* make it there? What if Martha's pettiness the day before was the final tallying point that marked her for the Terrestrial Kingdom instead? What if Dell didn't handle her illness well and got kicked out at the last moment? What if Martha did make it to the Celestial Kingdom despite everything, and Susan had an affair ten years from now and eliminated herself from consideration?

The sealing only worked if you *all* made it.

It was so confusing. Did being sealed at least give you visitation rights? Could you at a minimum get a passport and go down to the Terrestrial to visit your daughter once in a while? How about a visit to the Third World status Telestial Kingdom? How could the Celestial Kingdom be heaven if you could never see your children? And if you could in fact see them even if they weren't worthy, how did being sealed or not being sealed make any difference?

Maybe you *didn't* get to see anyone who didn't make it, but you were so busy creating your own worlds and having spirit children to people them that you didn't miss the family members who weren't strong enough to get there with you. Maybe it really did make a difference.

Martha wasn't about to take a chance. She got out her Sunday School manual and prepared her lesson for the 16- and 17-year-olds. She was a competent teacher, but perhaps she'd better start being brilliant.

Martha called Susan around 3:00. "Do you think you and Cliff could come for dinner tonight? We want to show we understand your decision and are behind you all the way."

"Really, Mom?"

"It was a very mature thing for you to do."

And Martha felt very mature now as well.

Not thirty seconds after they hung up, the phone rang, and Martha picked it up smiling, figuring it was Susan again, about to compliment her on her wisdom. "Hey, sweetie," she said.

"Honey, I need you to come over right away." It was Martha's seventy-four-year-old mother. She sounded deathly ill. Martha felt a cold shiver run down her spine.

"Are you all right? Should I call an ambulance?" Had her mother found out about Dell? Did she have cancer, too? What could be wrong? Martha couldn't handle another tragedy so soon. Not even the Church could give her that much strength.

"No. Just get here right away."

Martha jumped in the car and drove as quickly as she could without breaking the law. In ten minutes, she was pulling up in front of her parents' house on Mt. Olympus. There was a strange car out front. Was it a lawyer? Were they being sued for something?

Oh, my god. That wasn't the bishop's car, was it? Her seventy-eight-year-old father wasn't being excommunicated, too? This wedding must really be special, if Satan was fighting so hard to ruin it. Maybe Susan and Cliff were going to give birth to a future prophet. Maybe Cliff was on his way to becoming a General Authority himself. Martha had to be ready to accept a larger degree of tribulation, if it was going to help Susan.

But her heart was still pounding.

She rushed up to the front door, which opened before she could even knock. Her mother embraced her tightly, almost choking her, and sobbed and sobbed. Her father stood behind her, crying as well. Had Dell actually died already? She'd seemed reasonably well last night when Martha had talked to her.

"Come in," said Martha's mother. "You need to meet someone."

Martha entered the house nervously and followed her parents to the living room. "Dell? Is that you?" The woman looked like Dell, but there was something that wasn't quite right. What was going on?

"Martha," said her father, struggling as her mother sobbed again, "this is our daughter, Samantha."

Martha was floored. "What the—?" Her parents had given a child up for adoption? How could they? Martha weakly held out her hand, and the two women shook. Samantha looked imperious, making Martha feel uncomfortable.

Wait a minute. Was the woman blackmailing her parents? Her father hadn't introduced Samantha as Martha's sister. Had she been born out of wedlock? Was she not sealed to the rest of the family?

No, that couldn't be. Samantha clearly wasn't as old as Martha's older siblings.

"Samantha," her father began. "Samantha..."

"Martha, you and I were switched at birth," the woman said bluntly. "I found out accidentally a couple of months ago that I wasn't genetically related to the people who raised me. Thank heavens. I did some research and found that you were born at the same hospital at almost the exact same time as I was. I got a lawyer to force your parents to take a blood test, and the results came back today. These are my parents." Samantha motioned to the old couple. "I expect you belong to the couple who raised me."

Martha stared with her mouth open. Time seemed to stand still. Martha had never understood that phrase before.

"We still love you, Martha. You'll always be our little girl."

Martha felt a chill, colder than anything she'd ever felt. She *wasn't* their little girl, she realized. She was born under the covenant to another family. *This* woman was automatically sealed to Martha's family, even never having met them all. Martha might be theirs legally, perhaps, but spiritually she belonged to someone else, people she might not even like. This was all a hellacious cosmic joke.

Her parents were old. After a couple more years, she might never see them again. She might never see Dell again. She might—

No, Susan was hers. Martha's marriage to Don was legitimate, even if Martha had just lost the rest of her family.

"What do your parents think of this?" Martha asked Samantha weakly.

"*These* are my parents," she repeated. "You mean what do *your* parents think. *Your* father was stake president. *Your* uncle is a regional rep. *Your* only sister is married to a bishop." She laughed. "They're all bastards. But they're yours forever now. You're certainly going to a 'good' family." She laughed again.

"She's not going anywhere," said Martha's father.

"I don't want her at family dinners," said Samantha stiffly. "Those are for *family.*"

Martha's mother sobbed again.

"Martha," said her father gently. "We'll adopt you."

"Nope," said Samantha curtly. "Her parents want her for themselves. You can't take away a child that's sealed to someone else without their consent. Your hands are tied. She's out of here."

Martha and her parents looked at each other in anguish. "It—it's not like we *can't* see people we aren't related to in the Celestial Kingdom," said her father. "Surely, we aren't barred from seeing friends…"

"Friends?"

Martha's mother started sobbing again, and Samantha smiled. "Maybe," said Martha's mother hopefully, "maybe we can adopt Susan."

"Then *I* won't have her in the next life," said Martha. She suddenly felt a tremendous rage and wondered if killing Samantha would exclude her from the Celestial Kingdom.

"Perhaps you ought to leave," said Samantha with a slight smirk.

"Martha is always welcome here."

"I don't want her here while I'm visiting *my* parents."

Martha nodded and walked out listlessly. She got in her car and headed home in a daze, going well below the speed limit but still running one stop sign without seeing it. The truck that rammed into the driver's side of the car had no time to brake.

There was a terrible tangle of glass and steel, and Martha stared dully through the wreckage as she waited in searing pain for help. She felt wet and sticky, and she smelled gasoline. Who would come to meet her in the hospital, she wondered. She couldn't see her body but could feel blood flowing freely from it, and she started to grow cold. The feeling she'd experienced at her parents' house seemed to be becoming permanent. How could her biological parents claim her in the next world if they'd never even seen her once here? How could the parents who had raised her claim her if she wasn't sealed to them? Was she to be an orphan throughout eternity, caught like Tarzan between his human family and his simian one and belonging really to neither?

Martha remembered a time when she was ten and had been ill with scarlet fever. Her mother had sat by her bedside for hours and hours, every day for a week. The woman had rubbed her down with damp washcloths, with alcohol wipes, had sung to her, had read her stories. She'd even started reading *Little Women*, knowing it was a classic girl's story, not realizing what was in store for Beth. Martha remembered how her mother had stopped reading after making up something about Beth's miraculous recovery.

But miracles *did* happen. At least to faithful Latter-day Saints. And God would perform a miracle now. He'd let Martha be with the family she loved.

"Remember, what is sealed on earth is sealed in heaven," Martha remembered hearing during General Conference. Could you be spiritually sealed without being physically sealed?

If love were enough to seal someone, though, who would need the temple?

She was trying to make sense of everything, but she was so very, very tired.

Then Martha had another thought. If she died now, she could still go to the temple as a spirit and witness her daughter's wedding, after all. Maybe Samantha had done her a favor. She wouldn't be with her daughter for the next twenty or thirty years, but what really mattered was all the time after that.

"Please don't let me be rescued," she whispered. She was afraid her murderous thought about Samantha earlier would damn her, but she was too tired to repent and face life without her entire family. She wanted to go to the temple. She wanted to sit with Susan and Cliff in the Celestial room.

Martha's hand could only reach her leg. She felt a thick, waxy substance there. Maybe the clots would seal her wounds. Or had her seal to life been irrevocably broken along with the seal to her parents and siblings and grandparents and cousins?

She felt she'd just been excommunicated. If she lived, she would have to invite Cliff's father over, make him feel he was still part of the family, even if he really wasn't until he repented and was rebaptized.

Martha couldn't go backwards, but maybe she could still go forward.

All those generations of genealogy which meant nothing now. All that hell of doing endless hours of research. All those

Books of Remembrance. All those hours in the temple doing sealings for people who belonged to another family. Yes, she'd helped needy people to be blessed with the eternal bonds of matrimony, but what good did that do *her* now?

Then Martha had another horrible thought. What if Susan had been switched at birth, too? What if Susan wasn't really sealed to her, either?

She cried out weakly and heard someone bang on the metal of the car's hull. Martha had lost the feeling in her legs and hands, and now she closed her eyes and tried to sleep.

"Hang on, ma'am, we're almost there," said a voice outside the wreckage.

Martha could barely hear the voice, but suddenly, there was a loud "whump" and lots of excited shouting. She didn't quite know what all the fuss was about. Then through her closed eyelids, she could see a bright flickering. She opened her eyes. There was light everywhere. It was a very hot light, but maybe this was the entrance to heaven. Was she supposed to go into the light?

But maybe since she had no family waiting for her on the other side, she was destined instead for hell. "We are saved or damned as families," she remembered hearing once in Sacrament meeting.

The feeling seemed to come back to her body, and as the hot light grew nearer, Martha finally realized what was happening. She began screaming and screaming, for Don, for Susan, and for her mother.

She died alone in her car, a small crowd gathered around to watch the inferno that engulfed her in her last moments. There was even a news crew there filming, having just happened along, so the scene could be forever preserved for posterity.

Working Out

Things were finally beginning to work out for Miranda. She smiled and peered through the blinds to the Time Saver across the street. She'd been fired from her job as a receptionist for an eye surgeon shortly after she'd moved into the apartment upstairs, undoubtedly because one of those mean girls at the nursing school had called to tell them she'd been kicked out. But then miraculously, the manager of the apartment complex told her she was quitting and asked if Miranda wanted the job. She passed the interview without hardly even flirting, moved into the apartment/office downstairs, was given free rent and utilities, plus was paid $800 a month. She'd been the manager for two months now without a problem, and maybe finally life was going to turn out all right. She wasn't quite sure if it meant God was finally blessing her, or if it was just luck.

There was a knock at the door, and Miranda opened it. A young woman about 23 was in the hall. She was blond and probably a size two. Miranda could tell instantly she was trash. She could always tell about other women. She had an easy guide. If she thought it was someone Keith would probably pick up on Bourbon Street, then the woman was trash.

"Can I help you?"

"I was wondering if you had any vacancies? For a one-bedroom?"

The last thing Miranda wanted was for a slut like this to live in the complex, but she got points for filling up apartments, so she couldn't turn her down. It seemed a bit flashy to want a one-bedroom instead of an efficiency, though. The girl probably had a sugar daddy. At least that meant she wouldn't come on to

Keith if they met in the hallway while Keith was over making one of his visits.

"Sure," said Miranda sweetly. "Come on in and fill out an application."

After the sleazy tramp left, Miranda put the application aside to give to the building owner later, and she got back to her work. She finished her typing and filing for the day, and then she pulled out her Thighmaster and exercised for a few minutes. She also had some five-pound weights she regularly lifted while on the phone, and some ten-pound weights she lifted maybe twice a week when she really felt in the mood to work out her frustrations. She wouldn't need that if Keith would just step up to the plate and marry her. She fasted twice a month for that, for how many years now? What would it take to convince God to bless her? She knew she just had to show God she was willing to endure to the end, and now that Keith was finishing school, she had done that.

Miranda's weight kept going up and down as she skipped meals and dieted and then ate fatty foods, but she was still a size fourteen, almost a sixteen, and at the age of thirty-two, there wasn't much chance of getting married if Keith didn't ask her. But he would. He was almost finished anesthesiology school and would be leaving New Orleans and moving to Alexandria for a new job after he graduated next week. He kept insisting he wasn't going to take her with him, but Miranda knew he would. And obviously the only way he could get her to go was by marrying her. Things were definitely looking up. Soon she could kiss this dead-end job good-bye.

Miranda squeezed some hand springs for a couple of minutes, but the handles were hard and hurt her fingers, so she put them down and looked out the window again. Keith had only come over here once during the daytime since she moved in, usually preferring the dark when no one would see him, but she kept hoping. Of course, that one time during the day hadn't been a very pleasant experience. She was on the phone last week with the exterminator for the complex, and Keith had barged in, furious from a letter Miranda had just sent him. He picked up pencils and pads from her desk and threw them at her as she talked on the phone, whispering, "I'll have your job! You wait and see! I'll get you fired for harassing me!"

But *he* was always the one who called, usually after 11:00, saying he'd be over soon to sleep with her. Though that wasn't the term he used. And like always, he ripped her clothes off as soon as he came in the door. She still couldn't bear to let him come in her mouth, and she refused to let him do anal sex to her, so almost every time they had sex, he criticized her the whole time. But he kept coming, didn't he? So Miranda knew he really loved her. Why else would he keep seeing her for sex after seven years, if he truly hated the sex?

He might actually try to get her fired, though, just so he could pretend he had to take her in because Miranda had nowhere to go. He wouldn't want people to think he loved her, after telling everyone for years he didn't, but he'd marry her, and she would know the truth. Once, he'd even let slip that he might take her as a wife, though he quickly joked that he'd keep her locked up in the attic, but it was too late. He'd let it out, and she knew how he really felt. And how could she ignore the fact that seven years was how long Jacob had worked to marry Leah, and that he'd worked seven more years for Rachel? Miranda had now worked seven years for Keith, and God simply had to hand him over. It was only fair.

There was another knock on the door. When Miranda opened it, she saw the creepy 35-year-old man who lived in B-

214. A few days ago when she'd left her laundry in the dryer and come back to her apartment to wait for it to finish, when she'd gone back, she found two of her panties missing. And the guy from B-214 had been walking across the parking lot then, pretending he didn't see her. She'd used her key to get in his apartment the next day when he was at work, but she didn't find anything. Still, she knew it was him. He probably sold the panties to a friend, or brought them to work to fondle during his lunch break or something.

"Can I help you?"

"I'm Bruce from B-214."

"Yes, I know."

"My kitchen faucet is leaking. And my garbage disposal doesn't work."

"Okay. I'll report it to maintenance."

"Thanks."

"No problem."

The man hesitated a moment, so Miranda didn't close the door. "You know," he said shyly, "you're the nicest manager we've had in a long time. I hope you stay a while."

"Thank you," said Miranda curtly, closing the door in his face.

So that's what happened to the panties. After that pervert had sniffed them or done some other ungodly thing with them, he'd put them down the garbage disposal. Why else would it be broken? Garbage disposals didn't just break. What a creep. And with that latest admission that he liked her, it was clear now he was stalking her. Men were just dogs.

But Miranda dutifully noted the complaints and called the maintenance guy to let him know about them. Of course, the maintenance man had leered at her a couple of times, too, so she didn't like him, either.

Miranda was about to turn and go back to her desk when she looked through the window and saw two men in white shirts and ties step out of a car in front of the Time Saver. She gasped and stepped back from the blinds but kept looking.

That was Elder Andrews! What was he doing here? She'd had a mild fling with the twenty-year-old Mormon missionary a few months earlier, while she was staying with her friend Bonnie right after being kicked out of nursing school. Bonnie had sex or at least petted with Elder Peterson, Andrews's companion, almost every night when the two missionaries came over at 10:30 to watch movie videos. They rented a room in the garage behind Bonnie's house. After a while, Elder Andrews had made his move on Miranda, and they kissed while the movie played.

But then Miranda found out he was really after Bonnie, and then Bonnie's mother had told him lies about Miranda, and it was all a big mess. Now Bonnie had moved to Utah to try her luck with Peterson, who had finished his mission, and so what was Andrews doing here? He knew she lived here; he'd helped her move. Was he checking up on her?

Then Miranda remembered the two elders she'd seen at the Time Saver a month ago. It was 10:30 at night when she first noticed them, and the rules said they were supposed to be in bed by then. But they went inside the convenience store and played pinball until 11:00, looking out through the window at Miranda's apartment the whole time. Around 11:30, they came outside and looked directly across the street. Then they'd looked disgusted, made a phone call, and left.

Had they been spying on her? Were they checking for the bishop to see if Keith came over? Had Keith been the one to get them to spy on her? Was he really married, and it was his wife was checking up on him? Had Bonnie's mother said something? Was it someone from the nursing school? It could be anyone, but it was almost certainly the Church.

Years earlier when she'd been attending her ward, back when Keith was separating from his wife, Miranda had seen Karen leave the chapel with her baby once, leaving her purse on the pew. Of course, even then, while Keith was having an affair with Miranda, he had started nasty rumors about Karen that everyone believed, and Miranda had seen with her own eyes as the bishop's wife, who babysat for Karen's little girl, leaned over and looked through Karen's purse while she was gone. And while Miranda was staying with the Robertsons, Brother Robertson would say he had to go out on an assignment from the bishop and spy on some church member. So Miranda knew it went on.

Miranda had eventually forgotten about the two elders from a month ago, but what could she possibly think now? The elders went inside and played pinball, but they kept looking across the street. And she knew these two were aware that she lived here, whether the others last time had known or not.

Miranda sat on the sofa with her hand on her chest. What was she going to do?

She went to her desk and picked up the phone. Keith had forbidden her to call during the day or after 11:00 at night, but now that his classes were over, it wouldn't matter, so she dialed his number. The answering machine clicked on. "If you're a friend, leave a message. If you're not, I've got this place booby trapped. If you know me, you know it's true. Beep."

Miranda rolled her eyes. Every time she heard one of his stupid Rambo messages, she remembered the times they'd had sex at his place and she found either a knife or a gun under his pillow. He'd joked that they were there in case he ever finally got tired of her. She knew the purpose of life was to start on the pathway to perfection, and she marveled sometimes at how far Keith still had to go. He threw this same point in her face all the time, too. "We're supposed to be working toward perfection," he'd say. "If we're going to have eternal sex, you sure have a long way to go before you're perfect at it." But she wasn't concerned about any of that now. She had something important to tell him. "Keith, your spies are across the street. Give me a call."

She felt better then, glanced out the window again, and went back to her desk and found something to do. She liked to stay ahead of schedule in case her boss came to the complex to check up on her. The maid had been fired a couple of weeks back for leaving the vacuum cleaner in the hallway overnight, where it was stolen. Well, that was the *official* reason they gave, but Miranda knew that the maid had reported seeing the maintenance man with his pants down when she'd gone in to an unoccupied apartment. His back was to her, and when he heard the door, he zipped right up. The maid didn't know if he was just stuffing his shirt in or what, but she'd told Miranda, and Miranda had told her boss. The maintenance man was still here, and the maid was fired. That's the way it always was. Men simply got away with everything, and women paid the price. Miranda wanted to make sure she was doing her job well so they couldn't do that to her.

Keith didn't call back, but he showed up at 11:30, knocking abruptly on the door. Miranda was half asleep, and the first thing that came to her mind was that another drunk from the bar next to the Time Saver had come into the building. The first week after she'd become manager, some guy had pushed his hand through a window trying to get in, and then he'd bled all over the stairwell and the sidewalk. Men were such creeps. But after a moment, Miranda realized someone was calling her name.

Her eyes opened wide and she leaped off of the sofa and hurried to the door. Keith hated to be kept waiting. He didn't like anyone seeing him in the hall. She undid the chain and let him in.

Keith shut the door, locked it, and then stood staring at Miranda in her pajamas, with an odd look in his eyes. "What the hell is going on?" he demanded.

"There were two missionaries across the street. They stayed out there for two hours. I was just wondering if you sent them to check up on me."

Keith put his hand on his forehead and shook his head slowly. "And what would I be expecting to find while you're at work?"

"I don't know. They were out there till 11:30 one night. They might even be out there right now." Feeling a sudden thrill, she rushed to the window and looked out, but the elders were gone. She knew that Keith denied to everyone he was seeing her. She wished someone else could find him here to back her up.

"Well, since I'm here, take off those clothes," said Keith.

"No," said Miranda, sitting on the sofa. "Let's talk first. We never talk. I want to tell you what I read in the Book of Mormon this week." That should cool him down for a couple of minutes.

Keith sighed. "Take off the clothes or I'm leaving."

Miranda looked down at the floor. She knew he would, but she also knew she only had a week left to work out a way to get him to propose. "You just need to get me in the mood is all. You know it takes women a little longer." Why was he always so mean? Why was he pretending he didn't he understand?

He walked over to the sofa, and standing before her, he unzipped and pulled out his erect penis. She felt like dirt and wanted to hit him. Then he put his hands on the back of her head and pulled her forward. "This will get you in the mood." She resisted, but he pulled her forward again.

He was gone twenty minutes later, and Miranda put her clothes back on. She lay on the sofa and looked at the slivers of the Time Saver sign she could see through the blinds. One more week, she thought, before he graduated and left New Orleans, and yet Keith sometimes waited two weeks between visits. She'd have to come up with some special way to get him back over. Thinking of different plans she might try, she slowly fell asleep.

Miranda woke up with a smile, knowing now how to get Keith to come back over. She'd tell him she joined a health club. He'd see she was seriously trying to lose weight, and he'd come to see her again. He was horny all the time. It wouldn't take much.

She had, in fact, been thinking a great deal about joining a gym. After all, there was one just a couple of blocks away, the big one that the Metairie bishop owned. The fact that a Mormon owned it was what kept her from joining sooner, but now that was something in its favor. She wanted the Church to see that she was a strong, independent woman who didn't need them or a man to make her happy. And if Keith ever came by the gym to see if she were really working out, they'd see that he *was* interested in her, despite what he told everybody. Maybe the bishop himself would even be there to see Keith. It would be wonderful.

At 5:00, as soon as Miranda got off work, she walked down the street to join. It cost a good bit, she realized, irritated that the bishop was probably a millionaire. The Church always seemed to get successful businessmen to be their leaders. That was why there was no spirit in church. It was run like a business. A business that always favored men. And she hated herself for giving her own hard-earned money to a rich Mormon when she still had $200 in NSF checks to pay back to the bank from when she lost her last job. But this was an investment that would pay off quickly, so she went in and worked out for half an hour.

Miranda was still wearing her make-up since she'd just gotten off work, but no one at a health club would be interested in such an obviously out-of-shape woman, so she didn't even look twice at the men. There was that grotesquely fat man over there, but even if he was interested, Miranda certainly wasn't. And that other guy wasn't too out of shape, but God, he was ugly. Then a cute guy glanced in her direction and smiled, but Miranda immediately looked away, not wanting to see the disgust and rejection in his face when he finally got a good look at her. Besides, she realized, he wasn't really all that attractive, after all. There were few men really who were as good looking as Keith. His hair was starting to thin a little these days, and she hated bald men, but she'd put so much into this relationship already that she didn't feel she could give up now.

She'd gone out on one blind date while she was living in the nursing dorm, hoping to make Keith jealous, but the guy had turned out to be a real dork, and at the end of the evening, he admitted he had a girlfriend waiting for him at home. Most of the male nursing students were gay, so they were out of the question, and who did that leave? Miranda didn't really know how to meet other guys, and what other way was there to make Keith propose? She wasn't about to go to a bar, she'd die before she went to a Singles meeting at church, only losers used personals ads or went to Matchmaker, and she wasn't allowed to date anyone in her building, so what else could she do? She tried to do her grocery shopping right after work while she was still dressed nicely, hearing she could meet some guys there, but only one guy had ever looked interested, a slimy looking Italian guy with gold chains and his shirt half unbuttoned, who squeezed some melons while smirking creepily at her. He made Keith seem like a gentleman. She wondered sometimes why she put up with Keith, but he really was about the best thing out there, and she knew she'd never really love anyone else.

Keith never used condoms, but Miranda still never managed to get pregnant, though she'd told him several times, of course, that she was. She wondered if something was wrong with her and she'd never get pregnant, or if God was just waiting for the right moment. She'd felt sure if she became a nurse like Keith was that he'd want her, but when she'd called in tears after failing her pharmacology test and being kicked out, he'd just said coldly, "I knew you were too stupid to make it." He'd *promised* to help her study when she enrolled, but he never did, not even once. And now he was going to be making even more money as an anesthetist, and he said that even a nurse didn't make enough for him to marry anymore.

He'd probably still screw around even if they were married, of course. He'd screwed around on Karen, and he said he was having sex with other women anesthetists and women doctors now. But as long as Miranda got to be #1 by being his wife, everything else would be okay. It would definitely be better than living alone Besides, once they were married, she'd find ways of keeping him home. She wasn't stupid.

After exercising for half an hour, Miranda walked past the rows of other people working out and strolled back to her apartment. As she reached the Time Saver, she decided to go in and buy a Coke, but as she walked in the door, she realized the two elders were in back playing pinball. She surely looked frumpy after the exercising, but at least she still had on some make-up. She walked up and down the aisles, pretending to be looking for something, trying to get close enough so that Elder Andrews could say something to her, since she wasn't about to make the first move.

But as she walked nearer, out of the corner of her eye, she saw the two duck down and hide. So they *were* spying! They weren't here just because they had an apartment down the street, like she had considered. They probably lived miles away. They were clearly here for her! She stopped in her tracks, wondering what to do now. Then she heard them giggling. That seemed rather odd.

"She must be crazy!" she heard Elder Andrews whisper. "After what she said about me!" And the two young men giggled again.

Miranda tried not to look as if she heard them and instead quickly walked up to the counter with her Coke and left. How could he say that? She wanted to run back to her apartment as fast as she could but made herself walk slowly so they wouldn't think anything was wrong. She kept hearing Andrews over and over in her head, and as soon as she closed the door behind her, she threw the Coke in the sink, where the can split and brown liquid fizzled everywhere, and she opened her mouth in a cry that never came out.

Why had he said such a thing? What could it possibly mean? She'd never said anything at all about him. Bonnie's mother must have told him more lies before he was transferred over here. Why did people do this to her all the time? What had she ever done to them? They treated her like she was a freak. What in the world was wrong with everybody?

She looked at the Coke spilled everywhere and closed her eyes. She'd have to call Keith and tell him what Elder Andrews had said.

Suddenly, she opened her eyes again and smiled. Why, yes, that would work out just right, she thought, smiling even more broadly. She'd call Keith to tell him about the missionaries, and she'd only mention in passing that she was on her way home from the gym. That way, he'd hear about the gym without thinking she was trying to impress him. Why, that was perfect, she realized. That would be even better than she'd hoped. He'd feel sorry for her, come over to comfort her, plus see that she was trying to get in better shape. Only six more days, but she'd get him. And she'd make up something about a businessman in a suit in line at the check out counter flirting with her, perhaps dangerously so, just to make sure she caught Keith's attention.

Miranda almost skipped to her phone and dialed. As she listened to Keith's recorded message, she wiped her smile off and tried to get in the right mood again. She tried to sound frantic, almost suicidal, as she told the machine what had happened. Then she hung up and sighed happily. She hummed a little tune as she walked back to her kitchen to clean up the mess.

She tried to do a little extra cleaning around the apartment, too. Then she took a shower and put her make-up on again, even though applying it took ninety minutes, so she'd be ready when Keith showed up in the middle of the night. She even skipped dinner tonight to lose a few extra ounces. Keith would see. With the proper incentive, she could be a great person. She'd be absolutely wonderful if only he would just marry her. And he *would* marry her, soon.

Yes, she thought happily, straightening up the Church books on her bedside stand. Things were finally working out just fine. Men were pigs, and God was a man, but even God would have to come around and bless her eventually. She had six days to enact her plan. God had made the world in six days. Miranda could make a husband. Keith thought she was stupid, but she'd show him she was smart enough to get what she wanted. He'd never even know what hit him. She rehearsed in her mind how to casually describe the businessman at the Time Saver so it would sound like she wasn't even really thinking about that part of her encounter in the store. She wished there were someone she could call to confide in about what she was doing, maybe rehearse with them a little. But she didn't know anyone. So she prayed instead.

"God, I realize you're a man, but you're a *perfect* man, so I know you understand." And she smiled, sitting on the edge of her bed, waiting for the wonderful night to come.

Twenty-six Years

Susan wanted to see it. She couldn't believe it was even here in a video store in Hattiesburg. Small towns in Mississippi weren't known for progressive thinking, even if they were university towns like hers. Susan glanced down again and, looking around to see that no one was watching, she picked up the DVD. *Latter Days*.

Alan would be upset if he saw she'd rented it. He was more homophobic than she was. She'd been shocked ten years ago when her nephew, Jeff, had told her he was gay and had been excommunicated, but she still loved him. Alan always told her in private that he knew Jeff was going to hell, though he was always nice to Jeff in person. Susan didn't know if he was going to hell or not. Probably he was, but she didn't treat him any differently now that she knew. She could be open-minded.

Susan decided she'd have to watch *Latter Days* sometime before Alan came home from work. Maybe tomorrow she'd teach half a day and then go home sick. She could watch the movie alone before Laura, her youngest, got home from high school. Anna was in college now and rarely around the house, and the two oldest children had married in the temple and lived away from home. She'd be safe.

When Susan reached the head of the line, she put the two DVDs she was renting on the counter. The other movie was *Kate and Leopold.* The clerk, a bored-looking girl about eighteen, scanned the DVDs. "It's for a project," Susan explained, meaning the gay movie. Then she felt like an idiot. The girl didn't say anything but put the two movies in a bag for her.

Out in the parking lot, Susan slipped the DVD of *Latter Days* into her purse and left the other in the bag. She hoped the second movie would be okay. Laura and Anna were too big for things like *Stuart Little* and *Shrek*, so it was hard to find movies they could watch as a family. *Kate and Leopold* was fairly innocuous. It was a love story, and Susan had seen it at the theater by herself a few years ago, unable to resist Hugh Jackman. She didn't remember there being a sex scene. One hardly paid attention any more, but she wanted her girls to wait until marriage as she had, so the less temptation the better. Movies too often made sex seem like fun, and that wasn't good for married people, much less kids. That was why the Church forbid R-rated movies even for adults.

Back home, Susan quickly cut up some fresh broccoli and lightly cooked that in the microwave while she boiled some spaghetti and heated some Ragu. Alan had served a mission in Milan 28 years ago and wanted pasta at least twice a week, and the kids never seemed to mind. Her oldest, Steven, had gone to Peru on a mission. He was now second counselor in the ward bishopric, not bad for a 25-year-old, but Susan still thought him just as immature as before his mission, even with a baby daughter now. He'd just graduated from college and gotten his first real job as an accountant. He seemed like he'd have a good life, though, and that was a relief.

The oldest girl, Becky, had said all through her teens that she would also serve a mission, but Susan had known that would never happen. She liked boys too much. Susan's biggest disappointment was the year Becky went to New Orleans for Mardi Gras and came back drunk. As far as Susan knew, though, it was the only time she drank. Becky soon married in the Baton Rouge temple like her brother, and she'd just finished nursing school and moved to St. Louis to work in a critical care unit there. Susan wished Becky could have stayed closer to home, but St. Louis was where her husband got a job, so that's where they went. No kids yet. Susan hoped they wouldn't wait too long. After all, having children was more important that being a nurse.

Susan set the table and called the others in for dinner. Even though Anna was in college now, she still ate dinner with the family, which was nice. She had friends from a sorority, and Susan suspected that Anna had gone drinking with them a few times, but she'd never come home drunk, so that was something. She'd dated a nonmember for several months and gotten him to join the Church, but then a few months later she'd dumped him. Yet Susan still had hope she'd marry in the Church. An eternal marriage was the single most important thing you could do in this life.

"Spaghetti!" said Alan, sitting down a moment later. "Looks good."

"And broccoli!" said Laura. It was one of the few vegetables she liked.

"I always aim to please."

"Your turn to say the prayer, Anna," said Alan. They all bowed their heads while Anna offered a blessing on the food.

"Anything interesting happen today?" asked Alan. The question was directed to no one in particular.

Susan wasn't about to mention that she'd rented what was probably an anti-Mormon film, but that fact so overwhelmed her that she could hardly think of anything else to say. She forced herself to think of the fourth grade class she taught. "One of my students misspelled his name again."

"What's new?" said Anna. She swallowed a piece of broccoli and then added, "I gave another speech in speech class today. The other students get so scared, but I've been giving talks in church all my life, so it's no big deal."

"Well, we don't learn chemistry at church," said Laura, "and I'm studying my brains out just to make a B. I hate it." Laura was in eleventh grade and wanted to graduate in the top 3% of her class next year like her siblings had all done. She generally made A's and was never happy with a B, and that made Susan proud. The public schools here were not all that demanding, she knew, but an A was an A.

"Science is good," said Alan. "You can always get a job in the sciences." He himself worked with computers at the university. He didn't really like it, but their kids all received free tuition, so Susan knew he planned to stay until Laura graduated college.

"Who wants a job in chemistry?" asked Laura.

"You could do drug research," said Alan. "You know Grandma is always in pain because of her arthritis. You could develop better pain medicine. Or you could develop treatments for cancer. Or find a cure for AIDS."

"Who wants to find a cure for AIDS? 99% of the people who have it get it from sinning."

"So you'll let the other 1% die for spite?" asked Alan. Susan knew he didn't really care about people with AIDS, either. When Jeff told them a few years ago he'd contracted HIV just before he met Devon, Alan had been sympathetic in person but had afterward told Susan, "The wages of sin is death." He was challenging Laura now simply because he liked to play devil's advocate to keep the girls sharp. She liked that about him.

"I just think there are more important diseases to cure first."

"So you're saying drug research is a possibility?"

"Oh, good grief."

They went on to talk of other things. Anna talked of a boy in one of her classes who kept asking for help with the coursework. She couldn't decide if he was interested in her or just really stupid. Alan talked of having to instruct a professor yet again on how to use Blackboard to post assignments for his students.

Susan had nothing to offer. After three years as Relief Society president, she now had no callings at church, for the first time in as long as she could remember. So that took away lots of topics for conversation. And teaching was always just the same old thing. They'd found a knife in one of her students' backpacks last week, but that was old news. One of her fellow teachers was discovered to be having an extramarital affair with the school nurse, but Susan didn't want to say anything that might make the girls think about sex. She wanted to talk about the movie in her purse, which would be even worse, so she didn't dare.

As the girls were clearing the table, the phone rang, and Susan answered it. "Hi, Sharon," she said, recognizing her friend's voice. Sharon taught in the room next to Susan's.

"I don't know what I'm going to do!" moaned Sharon into the phone.

"What's wrong?"

"Someone shot at our house. I'm sure it was because of Kenny." Kenny was Sharon's teenage son who was into drugs. Thank God Susan had the Church and didn't really have to worry about things like that.

"Was anyone hurt?"

"No. Just a hole in the front door. Susan, I can't take this much longer. What am I going to do?"

Kick him out, Susan wanted to say. That's what she'd do if someone in her family was breaking the law. It would be a sign of love. Tough love, maybe, a little cold, perhaps, but still love. "Can you get him into rehab?" Susan asked.

"He won't go. I'm afraid he's going to get Pete into drugs." Pete was Sharon's 12-year-old.

"Sharon, you have to do something. You could get killed. Pete could get killed." Susan felt a little flushed to be saying this, watching the reaction of her girls as they overheard her end of the conversation. It was terrible the way lives could fall apart so easily without the Church. But it gave her a kind of thrill to be so near it. Near but far. Maybe she was getting too close by renting that movie. But she'd worry about that later.

"Oh, you're right," said Sharon. "What in the world am I going to do?"

"Did you call the police?"

"Oh, I can't! They'd want to know why someone was shooting at us. They might search the house. God only knows what they'd find in Kenny's room."

"Can't he go live with his father?"

"His father doesn't want him. That's why he's into drugs in the first place."

They talked a few more minutes, but there was really nothing useful Susan could suggest. "Tell him to repent!" she wanted to say. Kenny wasn't even nice. You could put up with a lot of sin if the person was at least nice. It made her want to be doubly sure her girls were safe, so after she hung up, Susan talked about how bad drugs were, without actually coming out and asking if Anna and Laura had ever tried them. You couldn't act suspicious, or that might drive kids away. But both girls made appropriately disapproving comments about drugs, so Susan felt okay.

After everyone had moved to the living room, Susan showed them the movie she'd rented for tonight, and they all settled down to watch *Kate and Leopold*. It was pure romantic fluff, but it was sweet. Hugh Jackman stood up every time Meg Ryan left the table. Susan remembered that at the beginning of their marriage twenty-six years ago, Alan had opened the car door for her every day. That had lasted about three years before he gave it up.

"I wish I could go back in time like Meg Ryan," said Anna. "Men are such dogs these days."

"Men were—" Susan stopped herself. She'd almost said that men were always dogs, but that wouldn't sound right. So she said, "There are some good men today. You only need one."

"Is Hugh Jackman married?" asked Laura, laughing.

"Afraid so." Susan had learned that when she looked up his name on the web. It wasn't that she actually lusted after other men. She really wasn't interested in sex at all. She and Alan hadn't had sex in seven years now. But every once in a while a good-looking man did catch her eye. She didn't think of sex when she saw one, though. It was more like simply appreciating a nice work of art.

"Mom, you got a minute?" Laura asked later as Susan was brushing her teeth.

Susan spit into the sink and turned to Laura. "What's up?"

Laura looked at her feet and kicked at the floor. Susan's stomach knotted. It wasn't about sex, was it?

"You know you can tell me anything." Susan could feel her pulse beating faster, but she kept a blank face.

"Well…"

"What is it? Something at school?" Maybe someone had offered her a cigarette.

"No," said Laura. "Well, kind of."

"It has to do with a teacher?" Had someone made a pass at her? She'd kill him.

"No."

"With a friend at school?" Did some boy grope her in the hall? She'd kill him, too.

Laura didn't say anything, so it must have something to do with a friend. But what had happened? Susan liked that her kids had always been able to come to her, but sometimes it was like pulling teeth to find out things.

"What'd your friend say?" Better to start with "say" and then move on to "do."

"Well, she was looking for something in her brother's room. And she found some magazines."

Oh, Lord.

"It was these women doing all sorts of terrible things. It really upset Jennifer. She wants to know if she should tell her parents. What do you think?"

"She should tell them right away. Pornography is addictive. That boy will only get worse. No telling what will happen if he keeps looking at that stuff."

"But her brother'll get mad at her if she tells."

"He'll never be a good husband if he looks at that crap. Jennifer won't only be helping her brother. She'll be helping her brother's wife when he gets married."

Laura was quiet a minute. Susan didn't know if she'd been too harsh. That sometimes turned kids off.

No, kids liked to have limits. And you definitely had to limit sex.

But why was Laura so quiet?

"Mom?"

"Yes?"

"Why are guys so...so sick?"

"I think it's genetic," Susan said slowly. Then she frowned. "Or maybe their spirits are different to begin with, right from the pre-existence. I don't know. That's probably why men need the priesthood to begin with. They're weaker. Just be glad you're a girl. We get cramps, but at least we aren't..."

"Perverts," said Laura.

"Right."

"Mom?"

"Yes?"

"Dad's not like that, is he? And Steven?"

"No, they're not like that."

"What about cousin Jeff?"

Susan shrugged. Jeff and Devon seemed so clean cut except for the gay thing. Neither of them smoked or drank. She hoped Jeff wasn't depraved in addition to being gay. Somehow, he seemed okay. If it was anyone else, she'd be more judgmental. But she liked Jeff. They connected.

"I don't think so."

"I hope not, or I'll never speak to him again. Dad doesn't like him anyway."

"You better get to bed."

"Good night, Mom."

Back in her room, Susan put on her nightgown and watched Alan strip to his garments. She'd never approved of sleeping just in her Mormon underwear, but Alan always did it, even though he knew she disapproved. It irritated her. Tonight, she wasn't going to worry about it, though. In fact, once she was in bed, all she could think about was the DVD in her purse. She felt guilty for sinning, but there was something exciting about it, too. She had never smoked and never drank, but she had once gone alone to a coffeehouse and ordered a latte. It hadn't actually been all that good, but to taste it was still thrilling. She'd never told the bishop about it, but she'd skipped taking the sacrament the following Sunday.

Lying in bed, Susan thought back to the time she was Laura's age. She'd been a good student, too. And she'd always enjoyed church. She'd read the Book of Mormon cover to cover when she was fifteen, and she'd had a testimony ever since.

She'd never really considered going on a mission, but she knew she'd only marry a returned missionary.

She'd met Alan at Institute on the University of Southern Mississippi campus in Hattiesburg. He always participated in class and always knew the right answers. He had a good sense of humor and seemed overall like a decent guy. They'd become friends first and only later did Alan want to actually date her. He was always a perfect gentleman, and when he proposed, Susan knew she'd never find anyone better.

They'd gone to Washington, DC to get married, that being the closest temple to Mississippi back then. That was 26 years ago.

Susan still remembered their wedding night, surely one of the most awful moments of her life. Alan had climbed on top of her and started pumping away. It seemed to take forever and was getting more boring by the minute. Susan had been thoroughly confused. Wasn't this supposed to be exciting? Wasn't this supposed to be fun? Why all the warnings against premarital sex if it was so unpleasant?

When Alan finally finished and plopped down beside her, he'd asked, "Did you come?" Susan didn't even know what that meant. But when she finally figured it out, she felt not only disappointed but cheated. Not once in all their years of lovemaking after that had she ever experienced an orgasm. Susan wasn't sure if Alan just wasn't doing it right or if something was wrong with her. She thought of trying to masturbate to see if she could stimulate herself, to see if she was physically capable of a climax, but that would be sinning.

So she became less and less interested in sex as the years went by. Once, about nine or ten years into their marriage, she and Alan were in the drugstore and Alan jokingly pointed to a

36-count box of condoms. "We should get it for our year's supply."

"That's a three year supply," she had responded immediately, not wanting him to get any ideas.

Alan had pestered her in the beginning for more sex, but thankfully he'd gradually gotten used to the fact that there wasn't going to be much. Susan had wanted to cuddle at first, but it seemed cuddling was always followed by an attempt at sex, and when she had pointed this out to Alan, he'd looked hurt and started staying on his side of the bed. But after a while, Susan no longer missed the cuddling. Then had come the day seven years ago when Alan had come to her with the big announcement. He was gay. Just like Jeff. He hadn't ever had sex with a man and he wasn't going to, but it was a secret he didn't feel he could keep any longer. He simply wanted her to know.

Strangely, Susan didn't feel either shock or revulsion at the news. What she felt was relief. "Thank god," she told him. "Now we don't have to have sex any more."

She never thought of divorcing him. Why should she? He was a good man. He was Seminary instructor at church, paid his tithing, and was basically good to her. He had been a stake missionary for years and Gospel Doctrine teacher for a while, too. He'd never been ordained a high priest, which was a little disappointing, but he didn't like leadership roles, anyway. He still wrote regularly to the five people he baptized in Italy.

But she had to see that movie about the gay Mormon missionary. What if? What if Alan had "come out," as they called it, instead of marrying her? What if she'd married someone else? She had good kids. She couldn't complain there.

And that was saying something in this day and age. But she might have had good kids with someone else, too.

And really, she wondered sometimes if that was enough. Once, she'd learned about a woman in the ward who was raped years ago and became pregnant. The woman kept the baby and loved her, because the baby was innocent and deserved to be loved, and she always seemed happy with the girl, who was so sweet even as a teenager. But could having a child you truly loved ever possibly mean the rape was a good thing? Susan was glad to have helped save Alan's soul, but she still wondered if that meant it was right for him to have married her. Yet maybe if he wasn't going to be satisfied with a woman anyway, it was good that she wasn't interested in sex with him, either. Maybe they were right for each other. And she had to admit, knowing he was gay somehow made her life a little more daring, more dangerous. She wasn't like all the other women at church.

But Susan had often felt a little distant from Alan, good as he was. If she could feel close to Jeff, why not to Alan as well? She always smiled at church, and people thought she was happy. But what would it have been like to be with a man who fully loved her? Not for the sex. She didn't care about the sex. But just to really feel completely loved.

And maybe—what the heck—maybe the sex would in fact have been good. She couldn't help but feel she'd missed out on a fairly basic part of her earthly existence. Sex was all anyone ever talked about. It must be good. What would it have been like to enjoy it even once?

She sighed and turned over, still thinking, but eventually she fell asleep.

Around 5:00, Susan woke up thirsty. She thought about waiting till the alarm went off at 6:00 to get something to drink but then decided she couldn't wait. She was going to try to get out of bed without waking Alan but then saw that he wasn't in bed. He must have gone to the bathroom. Susan got up and walked toward the kitchen, but as she passed the den, she saw a light flickering.

She peeked in and saw Alan watching TV, the volume low. That was odd. He hardly ever had insomnia. Then she saw what was on the screen. Two young men were in a restaurant kissing. What the-- ?

Susan stood behind Alan and watched as the last few minutes of the movie unfolded. When the credits started rolling, Alan removed the disk and put it back in the case. Only then did he see Susan.

"How long have you been there?"

"A few minutes."

"I had an upset stomach. I couldn't find any Tums and so I looked in your purse."

"I was going to watch it this afternoon before you came home from work."

"No, I think we should all watch it tonight after dinner."

"You mean you want the kids to see it?"

"I think they should."

"Was there any sex in the movie?"

"Yes. There was sex."

Susan was silent a moment. "Okay."

"Someday, they'll have to know, one way or another."

"You think that's wise?"

Alan laughed. "Wise? Who knows? You've been very good to me for a very long time, but it's hard to live without love. I know it's wrong, but I just get so lonely. I'll try to wait at least until Laura is in college. Maybe no one will even want me. But I think at some point I'll have to try."

Susan nodded but didn't say anything. So this was it, she realized dully. She would be getting a temple divorce. She wouldn't be going to the Celestial Kingdom. You could get there by yourself, she supposed, but she knew she wouldn't. Somehow, even with all those years of work, she'd lost. She thought she'd feel a little thrill if this day ever came, but she didn't.

Then she wondered briefly whether if she started dating in the future sometime, if she might have to have sex with someone else.

"You okay?"

She nodded again, the corners of her mouth turning upward just slightly. "I'm thirsty," she said. "I'm going to get something to drink."

Zombies for Jesus

"**D**o what you're told," Cliff said to his fifteen-year-old son, Jon, who was pulling the covers over his head. Cliff leaned over and ripped them back off.

"But Dad," said Jon, sitting up, "I hate Seminary. Everyone walks around in a daze all the time half-asleep. I gave it a year as I promised. I don't want to do it any more."

"We all do things we don't want to do. You think I want to go to work every day?"

Jon rolled his eyes. "But Dad, you *have* to do that. I don't have to go to Seminary."

"You do if you want your allowance."

"Jeez, sometimes you make me wish I was dead."

"You will be soon enough. Life is short. It's eternity we have to worry about."

Jon rolled his eyes again.

Cliff walked out to the kitchen, irritated. Did Jon think he liked teaching early morning Seminary himself? Cliff didn't have to be at work at the university until 9:00, and the Church was making him get up at 5:30 every morning so he could teach the teenagers at 6:00. Cliff hated teaching, which was why he'd gone into Information Technology in college in the first place. He hated teenagers, too. Sometimes, that even included Jon, his oldest. And ever since his time as a missionary, he hated waking up early. The kids weren't the only ones walking around in a daze.

But the bishop had called Cliff to this position five years ago, so what could he do? A call from the bishop was a call from God. Cliff couldn't let Jesus down.

Of course, today Cliff had more important things on his mind than the early Church history he was teaching. It was all fine and good that tens of thousands of people had followed Brigham Young across the plains without a second thought. Cliff was facing a layoff at work today, and getting laid off would definitely require a second thought from him. Maybe even a third as well.

Cliff had followed Mormon teachings faithfully his whole life, of course. Surely, God wouldn't abandon him now. Although there were a hundred layoffs to be announced at the university today, there would be only one layoff in Cliff's department, and God wouldn't let it be him.

"Hurry it up, Jon," Cliff called out as he drank his orange juice.

"Good grief, Cliff," said Elizabeth, his wife, walking into the kitchen, still groggy. "You're going to wake the dead. The rest of us don't have to get up at this ungodly hour, you know."

"Sorry." Cliff wasn't too sympathetic toward Liz and the other kids sleeping in. After Liz got the kids off to school, Cliff knew she always went back to sleep for another hour. She'd resisted the Church pushing her to be a stay-at-home mom when they first got married, but after a few years of it, Liz had resigned herself to a rote existence. Cliff resented that she still found ways to take it out on him, though. He'd have loved to have such a carefree life of his own, napping whenever he wanted.

In class this morning, Cliff told the students about the wagon train that had set out across the plains too late in the season, against the prophet's directives, and become bogged down in the snow. "Thus we see how important it is to follow the instructions of our leaders," said Cliff.

A hand shot up. "Brother Carlyle," said Andy, a friend of Jon's. "Didn't God want the Saints to get out to Salt Lake quickly? I mean, if they have to wait an extra five months in Illinois before going, who benefits from that? Couldn't God just have kept the snow back another couple of weeks?"

"There are natural laws we have to live with," said Cliff.

"Are you telling me God can't control the weather? I thought He split the Red Sea. I thought He brought the seagulls to Salt Lake to eat the crickets. I thought He brought earthquakes upon the Nephites. Can't God do anything He wants?"

"The prophet had spoken," Cliff said. "That was God's way of saying to do it that way."

"You mean God let those pioneers die just so the prophet could save face and be right?"

Cliff sighed. Teenagers, he grumbled to himself. They thought they knew everything. "We don't question God's actions."

"Then how do we understand Him?"

"We don't delve into the mysteries. The prophet tells us to stick to the plain and simple truths of the gospel."

"So we have to be mindless sheep?" asked Andy. "I thought the Church's motto was 'the glory of God is intelligence.'"

"I'm tired of this discussion," said Cliff. "Let's get back to the lesson."

He did return to the manual, but Andy's words irritated him, sticking into his mind like a splinter in the skin of his finger. There'd been a time when Cliff believed that intelligence was a good thing. He'd worked hard in school, naturally, but it was more than that. He used to read books about Lincoln and the Arctic and Henry the Fifth. He used to watch documentaries about the Louvre and continental drift and Native American Indians. He used to lie outside and look at the stars.

Packing up his teaching materials at the end of the lesson, Cliff wondered how long it had been since he'd read a book. With a full-time job and four kids, of course, who had time?

Then again, when was the last time he'd even thought about it? Cliff knew that as a god one day, he would have to learn *everything*. He used to want to start the process now. There used to be a time when he felt a person couldn't even inherit the Celestial Kingdom in the first place and have the privilege to finally learn all things unless he made an effort here to take advantage of every opportunity for learning that this life provided. What had happened?

Cliff drove Jon to school, not wanting to talk to him on the drive, still mad at his friend, Andy. Cliff remembered how after Liz had suffered so much during her pregnancy with Jon, she'd never wanted to bear any more children. Cliff had badgered her, repeating again and again how it was God's will, it was a commandment, it was an essential part of God's plan, it was what Mormons did. She'd relented unhappily, but it had resulted in far less sex for Cliff over the years.

We all do things we don't want to do, Cliff thought. Doing what you were told without asking why was the real ticket to heaven.

"See you, Dad."

Cliff grunted as Jon stepped out of the car.

"Have a good day at work."

"Yep."

Cliff drove off, arriving at the university an hour early, as usual. He logged onto the computer, but instead of playing a game as he often did, he checked the news. He hardly ever watched the news any more. There was fighting in the Congo, he saw now, a murder-suicide in Texas, and a volcano in the Philippines.

Boring.

Cliff was about to click back to his game, Zombie Killers, when he stopped himself.

Why was all that drama boring to him, he suddenly wondered. Then he wondered at the fact that he'd been able to wonder again. It had been a long time.

The flicker of life in his brain intrigued him. It reminded him of the time years ago when he used to dream of creating new inventions. Over the years, as he watched others come up with the MP3 and iPod and Wii and everything else, Cliff felt that life was passing him by. But he couldn't make himself sit down and study enough to do anything creative. Even just keeping up with the constant changes in computer technology was almost more than he could bear. Cliff wished he could simply relax and coast for a while. He was so tired all the time. He refused to take antihistamines because they made him feel foggy, but he had to admit, he felt foggy most of the time, anyway.

"Morning, Cliff," said his supervisor, Sandria, coming into the office.

"Good morning."

"Still getting here early?" she asked wryly. "Trying to ward off the evil eye of layoffs?"

"You know me. Can't wait to get to work every day."

Sandria laughed. "Well, there's a call here from Professor Ryan. Got locked out of Blackboard again. Can you go over and train him yet another time?"

"Sure thing."

Cliff hated dealing with Professor Ryan. He was first counselor in the stake presidency, and though Cliff was going out of his way to be patient with the man's Luddite tendencies, Ryan always seemed to be judging Cliff, continually making Cliff feel he was being reported on back to the stake president. Was he the reason why Cliff never got any real substantial calling at church? Was Cliff not conforming enough? Were all Ryan's supposed computer problems just chances at getting Cliff close enough to spy on?

"Hi, Brother Carlyle," said Dr. Ryan as Cliff entered the professor's office. "How's that early morning Seminary coming along?"

"Fine."

"Good, good." He paused, and there was an awkward silence. "Hey, got your garden planted yet?"

Cliff nodded curtly. He hated gardening, but it was a commandment to grow as many of your own vegetables as you could. He hated lots of things that seemed uniquely Mormon commandments. Cliff had dutifully researched his genealogy despite the fact that he found it utterly boring. He wrote in his journal regularly, though since he wasn't at all literary, the entries were less and less interesting as time went by. Some days, he just wrote about his latest Zombie Killer adventure. But he wrote, as he was told to do.

"Let's get you back up on Blackboard," said Cliff, trying to focus on business.

Before long, Dr. Ryan assured Cliff that he "got it this time," and promised to write him a good recommendation if he was laid off later in the day.

"You couldn't pray so that I won't get laid off to begin with?" asked Cliff. "What good is it to be close to God if you don't have any say?"

Dr. Ryan laughed but broke off when he saw Cliff wasn't laughing with him. "God can't *make* people be good and do the right thing," he said.

Cliff frowned. Why not, he thought. The Church forced *him* to do what it wanted all the time. He wore his white shirt to church every week, held Family Home Evening every Monday that his kids dreaded, home taught the families that put up with his visits for the same reason he made them, to check another item off the list of requirements for being a dedicated Mormon.

Cliff had been so excited to be sent to Alaska on his mission twenty years earlier. It would be exotic, he thought. He could see the way other people did things. But the Church had been exactly the same in Alaska as it was back home. People wore the same clothes to church, gave the same lame talks during Sacrament meeting, told the same faith-promoting urban legends. It was supposed to be comforting that the Church had a uniformity everywhere you went, yet Cliff found it oddly disturbing that all the members he ever met were all alike. He'd had three Jewish friends over the years, and they all believed different things. Their diversity hadn't harmed the Jews, who were part of what was surely one of the world's most enduring religions.

On his travels since, Cliff had tried to find comfort in the sameness of every ward he ever visited, but when he saw the remake of *The Stepford Wives*, he'd felt strangely uneasy. Mormons weren't programmed robots, he told himself. They were encouraged to study and pray and seek to know the truth for themselves.

But Cliff remembered how the elders quorum president a few years back had stood up in Fast and Testimony meeting. Most people who spoke during the monthly meeting seemed to be trying to convince themselves they believed and were happy, but this man stood in front of everyone and proclaimed that he had studied and prayed and been told by God that women should be allowed to hold the priesthood. He'd been pulled aside afterward and told he was allowed to ask God these things, but he was only allowed to get the same answer the leaders gave. Anything else was apostasy and was unacceptable.

The elders quorum president had eventually been excommunicated. He continued to attend meetings, but no one talked to him any more, afraid of being contaminated, as if he had some kind of viral infection that would turn them all into evil monsters. In the end, the man had stopped coming to church. "He felt too uncomfortable to be in our presence," he new elders quorum president said. "Sin will do that." Cliff had felt uncomfortable, too, but he quickly suppressed the thought.

"Okay, Dr. Ryan, give me a call if you have any more trouble."

"Sure thing, Brother Carlyle. Thanks a bunch."

Cliff walked out of the office, still irritated. The man was clearly brain damaged and would be calling again in a week or two. How did such a person ever get to be a full professor? How did he get to be a leader in the Church? How could any organization function with so many people blindly on autopilot?

Walking back to IT, Cliff passed several students in the hallway. One was a cute girl, probably a freshman. He smiled when he saw her but then stopped in his tracks when he read her T-shirt. "Be Happy. Be Mormon." He felt annoyed again.

Back in his office, Cliff did some paperwork. Then he was off another time to help an instructor with Power Point. Then he came back and played his computer game for a few minutes. After Cliff woke from his nap during lunch, Sandria came up to him and said, "It's time for us to start running our zombie check."

At first, Cliff thought she was referring to his game and felt confused. Then his head cleared as he became more awake. "I'll get right on it," he said.

The department periodically had to ensure that the university's computers were not zombies, hacked into and forced to perform unwanted tasks under remote direction. It happened all over the world, and with a network as large as theirs, the university was continually having to deal with viruses or worms or zombieism or some other hassle.

Around 3:00, all the IT personnel gathered back in the office for "the announcement." They'd decided they wanted to do this communally rather than have Sandria approach the lone victim while he was isolated in his cubicle.

"The decision was difficult to make," Sandria began. "You are all good workers, all intelligent, all dedicated. I feel I am friends with you all, and I didn't want to lose any of you. I had to take many things into consideration, and even then, I don't feel justified in letting any of you go. But in the end, I still had to choose somebody."

Everyone waited breathlessly, except for Cliff. He hated paying his tithing when the family was always struggling, but he'd paid it again just last week, so he knew he was safe. Besides, he'd been here longer than half the others. Nevertheless, it would be good to finally hear the actual verdict. Sometimes, God did do mean things for no apparent reason.

"Cliff, we'll do everything we can to see that you find another job."

God *did* do it! Cliff couldn't believe it. And yet somehow, he realized he'd been expecting it all along. God took you out in the desert and then abandoned you. He made you prophet and then let you be murdered in jail. He ordered you to have a family and then left you in misery with them for the rest of your life.

Everyone quickly dispersed, and Cliff stalked back to his cubicle and started gathering his things. Then he grew suddenly angry and marched over to Sandria's office. "Dead man walking," someone muttered.

"Why me?" Cliff demanded, standing in the doorway.

"I had to pick someone," Sandria said slowly, "and you spend more time killing zombies than actually working."

"Everyone plays games."

"But you spend more time in a trance in front of your computer than anyone else. You don't have any intellectual curiosity. I had to find some deciding factor. Now be a good boy and leave on your own so I don't have to call security."

The words stung brutally for a moment, and then all feeling ceased. Cliff turned around in a daze and plodded back to his desk slowly. He felt dead inside. How was he going to support his family now? How was he going to face everyone at church?

How was he going to face the rest of his life? He didn't think he could find another job in this economy. But he definitely didn't want to go back to school and learn something new. What was he to do?

Cliff knew that Sandria was right about his lack of intellectual curiosity. After beating himself into submission all his life, the only way he found he could make his spirit give in on so many issues was to force himself not to think or feel anymore.

Well, he was going to think now. Jesuits thought, didn't they? And the Catholic Church survived just fine. It *benefited* from their thinking.

That would never work in his own culture, Cliff realized sadly. He was destined to a lifeless life. His family were destined to remain undead zombies for the rest of their lives, too.

Walking out to the car, Cliff had a sudden thought. The Church squashed people's souls, pretending to save them. It wasn't unlike a voodoo priest "rescuing" someone from the grave, only to force them into slavery for the rest of their lives. But Cliff could find a way to *really* save his family's souls. Jon hated Seminary. Liz hated being Homemaker instructor in Relief Society. The younger kids hated Primary. They were all as bad as he was. None of them was going to make it to the Celestial Kingdom, despite giving in all the time to the Church's demands.

But Cliff could guarantee them access to the highest kingdom. He could make them martyrs. One bullet to the head for each of them tonight would do it. They were already brain dead, weren't they? And he'd had plenty of practice shooting on the computer.

It was Friday, so no one would miss them until Monday. He could even go to church on Sunday and help redeem more of the zombies there as well, bring them all to Jesus. They thought that being a zombie was enough to get them to heaven. It wasn't, Cliff recognized now, but he would see that they made it anyway.

Cliff was finally going to do something genuinely useful with his life. Something legitimately righteous. He might go to hell himself, but that was a small price to pay for helping so many others. Was it even murder, to kill someone who was only half alive?

Cliff threw his box of belongings into the trunk of his car, feeling a lightness in his soul he hadn't felt in years.

He drove home carefully, thinking about where he'd stored his ammunition. If for some reason he decided he'd made a mistake, he could always ask God to raise his family from the dead like he'd raised Lazarus. If worse came to worst, they'd still all be raised from the grave during the resurrection. It would all be okay.

After parking carefully in the driveway, Cliff carried the garbage cans from the curb back to the house. Then he let himself in through the kitchen door. He saw Liz plodding listlessly across the floor toward him, and he smiled brightly for the first time in days.

"What's for dinner, hon?"

"Tuna casserole with lime Jello for dessert." Cliff laughed and gave Liz a peck on the lips, startling her. What a perfectly Mormon last meal, he thought. He sat in his easy chair and turned on the TV. Some stupid judge show was on.

Suddenly, a horrible thought struck Cliff. What if the resurrection on Judgment Day didn't bring people to eternal life but everyone was instead forced to continue to serve unhappily throughout eternity? What if God really did want to make literal zombies of them all?

He sat there thinking furiously, and after a while, he realized with a shock that it was invigorating to be thinking so much. He was enjoying it.

Cliff looked to the kitchen, where Liz was still plodding slowly back and forth. Perhaps it was already too late to save anyone else, he reflected.

He'd have to think about himself for a change instead.

What did *he* want to do?

Cliff thought for a moment and then picked up the remote control. He flipped stations until he came upon the Discovery channel. There was a show on about African trypanosomiasis, sleeping sickness. Smiling, he sat back in his chair and watched as doctors talked about various treatments for the disease.

Maybe he could become a phlebotomist, Cliff thought. Or an X-ray tech. Something not too hard but which might still force him to think just a little. He could get a part-time job while he studied, and Liz could get a part-time job, too.

Jon burst through the kitchen door then and headed straight for his bedroom, but Cliff stopped him with a hand in the air.

"Yeah?"
"Just thought you ought to know you don't have to attend Seminary anymore."

Jon looked taken aback. "Really?"

"Really." He paused, wanting to say something more but not knowing what.

"You're not apostatizing, are you?" Jon laughed.

"Maybe I am," said Cliff carefully. "Would you have a problem with that?"

"Not if I can start seeing R-rated movies."

Cliff nodded. "I think it's about time. Pick something out and I'll go rent it for tonight."

"You mean it?"

"We'll have something for the other kids first, and after they're asleep, we'll stay up late and watch whatever you want."

"Hot damn!" Jon looked at Cliff guiltily. "Sorry."

"Curse all you goddamn want," said Cliff. "Things are going to change around here."

"Are you feeling okay?"

"Just regaining consciousness after a coma."

Jon looked at him uncertainly. "You're acting kind of weird, Dad."

"That's *fucking* weird, Jon."

Jon smiled, still a little unsure. "Okay, Dad." He continued on to his room, and Cliff went back to his documentary.

He was coming back to life again after many years in the grave, and he felt good. This time, though, there'd be no voodoo, no sorcerer to control his actions.

"You going to nap before dinner?" asked Liz, trudging into the room. "It'll be about half an hour."

"No," said Cliff. "No more napping. I'm off for a run."

Liz's eyes widened, and Cliff thought he saw a glimmer of life there, too. Perhaps she could be saved eventually as well. He gave her a kiss, surprising her again, and then headed out the front door at a brisk pace. He felt the fresh spring breeze on his cheeks, and smelled the mimosa in the air. Wondering what wild, stimulating movie was in store for him that evening, he broke into a run.

The Mark of Abel

Perhaps I should give you some background so you don't think I'm a complete asshole. I grew up in New Orleans in the 1960's, with frequent visits to the family farm in Mississippi. When the show *Julia* aired, I was forbidden to watch because it starred a black actress. When *Room 222* came on a few years later, that was off limits, too, because there was a black teacher.

Naturally, since the shows were forbidden, I watched whenever I got a chance. It wasn't reverse psychology—my parents truly did disapprove—but my reaction as a child was simply, "What's the big deal? So they're black."

We joined the Mormon Church when I was nine, and my parents relaxed into the all-white congregation. No blacks joined the Church in our area till after they were allowed to hold the priesthood in 1978. By this time, I'd been inoculated by *The Jeffersons*, so when my dad talked about "the new nigger high priest," I gently corrected him. He smiled knowingly.

After my mission to Chile, I attended the Spanish branch here in New Orleans, where I met my wife, Carmen, from Santiago. My parents were only happy to the extent that Carmen seemed pure Spanish and not a mestizo with Indian blood. Given that Mormons were celebrants of the Lamanites, I found their attitude odd. I never understood why Hispanics were classified as non-white to begin with. My sister was a lot darker than Carmen.

So life went on. After I earned my MA in English, I began teaching as an adjunct at both the University of New Orleans and Southern University at New Orleans. This was my first introduction to "separate but equal," thirty years after *Brown vs. the Board of Education.* Both were state schools, but SUNO was 99% black while UNO was largely white. The shocker for me was the difference in standards at these supposedly comparable schools.

At UNO, we were told to fail any paper that had three or more major grammar errors. When I did the same thing at SUNO, I was called in by the administration. "You have to understand where our students are coming from. You have to be more lenient."

So I began passing papers that wouldn't have stood a chance at the white school. Consequently, I was called back into the office. "You're trying to keep our students ignorant and in their place," was the complaint now.

I eventually found a "middle ground," only failing a paper if it contained more than fifteen major grammar errors. Sometimes, when there were just fourteen, I'd give an essay a D, and then I'd hear the complaint, "You can't give me a D, Mr. Andrews. I'm a high school English teacher." The student thought this revelation would impress me, not leave me appalled.

But the black attitude toward learning in New Orleans, that being educated was "trying to be white," was just one of the problems. By my third year at SUNO, I was receiving racist hate mail in my school mailbox almost every day. I thought maybe I'd inadvertently said something offensive in class, but when I talked to two other white instructors there, I learned they were receiving hate mail as well. "The white man is the devil" was one of my favorites. "Still making a living off of the hard work of blacks" was another. Some of the hate mail was even grammatically correct.

The clincher for me was right after the news reported how a white college girl from California had been mobbed and murdered in South Africa while trying to register blacks to vote. "White people always think we need their help," said one of my students about the incident. "They were right to kill her."

After ten years at SUNO, I was told point blank by one of the administrators, "I'm going to do everything I can to get rid of you because you're white," and sure enough, the next semester, my contract wasn't renewed. To be honest, it was a bit of a relief.

I can't say I *wasn't* racist. When my white friends and I would get together, we'd complain about New Orleans being the murder capital of the country. We'd moan about rap music, boys wearing their pants halfway down to their knees, about the "attitude" blacks gave whites in public, even gave each other. There was a popular bumper sticker in the city which read, "My child is an honor student." We joked about selling one that said, "My child be an honor student." I knew I was wrong to talk like this. We always prefaced our remarks by saying something like, "It's not blacks that are bad. It's the black culture that could use some improvement." But we knew we were prejudiced.

Really, though, I felt I hadn't become discriminatory *until* I began associating with blacks in an intensive way. I still corrected my dad when he used the N-word. I never spoke poorly of blacks in front of my children. I sustained the one black leader in my ward. I actually still even gave to the United Negro College Fund. Blacks might be receiving an inferior education, but I still believed some education was better than none.

Years passed. I left teaching and began working at the New Orleans Public Library, or as one of my coworkers called it "the public liberry." I was friendly with the black patrons and my black coworkers, and they were friendly to me. But when we ran into each other on the street, neither of us would talk to the other. I couldn't tell if they were embarrassed to be seen talking to a white person, or if they were worried that *I'd* be embarrassed to be seen socially with blacks.

None of my "best friends" was black, and I think I needed to make more of an effort in that arena. I noticed that when my friends at church told anecdotes, there were subliminal cues. "This loud black woman…" The story was about the woman being loud. Why did the fact that she was black have to be mentioned? "These two big black guys mugged me." Wasn't the mugging the real issue? Would it have been a more pleasant experience if the muggers had been white?

At the same time, on the news, there was an obvious lack of racial information. "A serial rapist has been stalking the Garden District. He is around thirty years old, 5'7", 160 pounds, with brown eyes." And was he white? Black? Asian? Sometimes, mentioning race was a clue, not an attack.

More than twenty years had passed since blacks were offered the priesthood, but the number of black Mormons in New Orleans was still pretty low. I was going to a "regular" ward with my family these days, mostly white, not Spanish and certainly not black. I could tell that people felt uncomfortable when new black converts would say "Amen" and "Hallelujah" in the middle of a talk. Cultural differences were significant. Assimilation made people feel better, and that wasn't entirely a bad thing.

Finally, that horrible day in August 2005 came that no one from New Orleans can ever forget. We'd evacuated but weren't allowed to return for a full month. What was left of our home in

Gentilly wasn't worth talking about. We made a decision as a family and headed to Seattle for a new start. God was with us, and both Carmen and I found jobs within a week. Victor, our oldest, had left on his mission to Norway from New Orleans and returned "home" afterward to a city he'd never seen. Our daughter Alice was just graduating high school and not ready to live on her own, so she came, too.

What happened to the 9th Ward was a tragedy. My father had built Fats Domino's house, which was now destroyed. But I began to resent that the hurricane was seen as a black disaster. I heard someone say, "New Orleans practices geographical racism. Rich, white people live above sea level while poor, black people live below it."

I found the accusation irritating. Did no one notice the near-complete destruction of Chalmette, a white, working class town? Did no one see that Lakeview, an upper class, white part of New Orleans, was right next to one of the levee breaks? My branch of the library there got ten feet of water. White people died in their attics.

Still, a year after the storm, I watched a retrospective with Anderson Cooper. He was in a boat near Tulane Avenue. On board was a white doctor. An elderly black man walked by in waist deep water. He'd been trapped in a building for days and finally decided to walk out. "This is criminal," said the doctor to Anderson Cooper.

"No, no. I got my I.D.," said the black man.

The unexpectedness of his protestation floored me. That this poor man had been so conditioned to being accused of wrongdoing struck me deeply, and I cried as the scene unfolded. Watching the rest of the program, I saw clearly that despite how many whites were affected, the slow response to the disaster was unequivocally the result of a racial reaction. Yes, thirty whites drowned in a nursing home, and two dozen more drowned tied to each other as they tried to walk to safety, but it was black bodies TV viewers saw floating in the water, black people huddled on their roofs, blacks living in squalor at the convention center. If something like this had happened in white Salt Lake, I had no doubt the response would have been different.

So was I a racist? Probably. I don't think it's possible for anyone of any race to grow up in this country without some degree of prejudice toward some other group. Mormons don't like Catholics, calling their church "the whore of Babylon." Catholics don't like Baptists. Baptists don't like Mormons. Democrats don't like Republicans. Everyone disliked someone. And if religious or political culture could be a reason for disliking someone, why couldn't ethnic culture?

Which brings me to my problem. While Victor was still only dating sporadically, yesterday Alice brought home her college boyfriend—Bekele. He was Ethiopian.

Bekele was a good-looking boy and polite enough. I told myself I didn't disapprove per se, that I was only concerned about the difficulties they would have to face as an interracial couple. Alice's children would be black, and they'd be caught up in African-American culture with all its problems. Did she know what she was getting herself into?

"Your parents didn't approve of my joining the family," Carmen reminded me.

"True," I admitted carefully.

"Our kids didn't suffer from being bilingual."

"No," I said slowly.

"You had the children stay with my parents in Chile every other summer, and they handled it just fine."

"Yes, but…"

"But?"

"But Spanish culture is European. We're cousins, not complete strangers."

"Bekele is our brother."

The next day at church, I asked the bishop's wife, Sister Parker, about her recent trip to South Africa. "African-Americans in South Africa are very different than here," she said quickly.

I was a little confused. "But what about the Africans themselves?"

"That's odd. You're calling them Africans. That's what they said, too. They didn't seem to like being called African-Americans. I wonder why?"

I stared at her. Sister Parker may have had a "good," white education, but she was still a ditz.

I had grown up hearing that blacks bore the mark of Cain, that they were cursed because they'd been less valiant in the pre-existence. That was all apparently inaccurate doctrine, but you couldn't fully erase years of racist teachings couched in loving terms.

I knew intellectually that there was nothing wrong with blacks. I knew in some respects the specificity of an Ethiopian-American culture was better than a generic African-American one. I knew that what I thought didn't matter in any event. Alice was free to make her own choices, and my not being supportive would cause us all more grief that anything we might receive from "society" in general.

Then I remembered another incident from my SUNO days. After the Rodney King riots, we discussed the fact that a white woman had been pulled from her car and beaten, though she was hardly a racist herself, married to a black man. "You can't indiscriminately attack all whites, assume we're all evil," I said.

"So you think her being married to a black man means we should be able to tell?" said one of my students in disgust. "You think contamination shows?"

I couldn't understand how she could take my call for tolerance as an insult. I realized then we were coming from such different backgrounds that perhaps it would never be possible to bridge that chasm. I decided to stop trying.

But years of ignoring the issue hadn't resolved anything, either. I needed to get over my residual prejudice overnight. How could I do it?

Carmen and I lived in Rainier Beach, considered the slums of Seattle, but no place in this city ever looked particularly dangerous to me after coming from New Orleans. Still, you could see blacks tossing trash on the street. That was another aspect of black culture I didn't much like. Then on my way home from work today, I stopped at Safeway to pick up a few groceries. It was my night to cook.

In the store, I noticed two fat black women eating a package of cookies they'd opened. Maybe they were going to pay for it later, but what they were doing still struck me as wrong. Two young black children were running up and down the aisles out of control. But I had seen unruly white kids before, too, hadn't I? In the checkout line, a black mother was yelling at her son, "You a no good piece of shit!" The boy wasn't even crying. He'd heard worse.

I walked slowly out to my car and started unloading my bags. One lane over, I could hear a thirty-something black woman shouting at a black man in his car. The woman was standing by the door gesticulating.

So low class, I thought, regardless of color. Could I really live with this? Was I going to feel prejudiced against my own family? What was I going to do?

Then something unexpected happened. The woman shouted, "If you hadn't been so adamant about it!"

Adamant? Really? Seattle obviously had a whole different order of low class people than New Orleans had. I actually smiled at the exchange.

"What are you looking at, asshole?" The woman had seen me.

"Don't sweat the small stuff," I said. I waved a friendly greeting and got in my car. I drove home, passing a black teenage girl in tight, hypersexual clothing.

The mark of Cain, I thought. Cain had hated his own brother. But maybe it was jealousy or bad feeling or prejudice itself which was a mark against someone, not their color. Racism wasn't always blatant. Sometimes, it could be subtle. Yet it was still racism. What I needed to develop was the mark of Abel.

I was clearly racist and would probably always be. I'd never been exposed to prejudice against Hispanics and hadn't had to overcome any of that. But there was no doubt a lot of work cut out for me here. I shrugged against my seat belt.

Having to work for something wasn't necessarily a bad thing, though, was it? Jacob had been forced to work for Rachel fourteen years before he got her, and that had worked out all right.

I pulled up in front of our house on 57th. Carmen was already home. I put the groceries on the counter and started chopping up some tomatoes. "We're going to have to change school night," I said as Carmen sneaked a chunk of tomato.

"Why? I like school night."

Every Tuesday, Carmen and I listened to lectures from The Teaching Company on any number of subjects. We were going through an astronomy course now. It's what Victor was studying in graduate school.

"We need to find out what language Bekele speaks and start learning it." There was a language school in town that had classes most weekday evenings. "Those kids are going to need to grow up trilingual."

"There are worse things in the world."

"Yes, there are."

"At least they can have a temple marriage."

Carmen sighed. "That's more than we can say about Victor."

"He'll find someone soon enough."

"He already has."

I frowned. "Really?" What was she talking about? "Why haven't we met the girl?"

"Samuel, sometimes you are truly dense."

140

I continued frowning.

"He's brought Philip over twice now."

"Huh?" Then the realization hit me. "Oh." My first thought after this was, "At least Philip is white."

Then I grabbed Carmen and hugged her and began laughing so hard I couldn't stop.

Hairdresser to the Gods

"**P**rochlorperazine is good for nausea," Nancy said to Sister Peterman as she trimmed off a finger of hair from her scalp. "Ask your doctor."

"Pro—what?"

"Prochlorperazine. I guess its common name is Compazine, but I find it easier to remember the chemical name."

"You're such a know-it-all, Nancy."

Nancy gritted her teeth and kept cutting. It wasn't the first time she'd heard the term. The other kids in school had thrown it at her all the time, and once, even a teacher had done so. Mrs. Kavanaugh, Nancy's sixth grade teacher, had just told the class about oil deposits and how they were formed. Nancy had raised her hand and asked, "So what do we do when the oil is all used up?"

Mrs. Kavanaugh had replied condescendingly, "There will always be oil."

"But Mrs. Kavanaugh, there is a limited number of organisms that have lived on the Earth. At some point, especially at the rate we're consuming oil now, there must be an end to the supply."

"You're quite a know-it-all, aren't you?" Mrs. Kavanaugh replied and then changed the subject.

The accusation mystified Nancy. She didn't know everything. That's why she asked so many questions. And what was wrong with knowing a lot? The Church said, "The glory of God is intelligence." But it also excommunicated her uncle

Mike, who'd taught at Brigham Young University, for being an "intellectual." It was all very confusing.

Nancy's parents risked the label of intellectualism as well. Not only did they encourage Nancy and her two brothers to get good grades, but they also routinely hosted foreign exchange students, to help those students, of course, but also to expose Nancy and her brothers to a larger world.

Nancy remembered Medha's visit. Shortly after the 16-year-old girl arrived from India, Nancy was showing her how to make sugar cookies in the kitchen. She used her special cookie cutters to give the dough shape. There was the cat, and the dog, and the cow, of course, but Nancy also had some dinosaur cookie cutters. They were living in the country just outside of Madison, Wisconsin, and Medha looked concerned when she saw the tin shapes.

"What's this animal?" she asked nervously.

"Oh, that's a T-rex."

"What's a T-rex?"

Nancy ran off to get her dinosaur book and soon returned with a drawing of the dinosaur in question. Medha's dark skin paled just a little. "And do—do you have many of them around here?" she asked. She looked toward the window worriedly. "Maybe with those little arms, they can't hurt us?" she asked hopefully.

It was only then that Nancy realized Medha had never heard of dinosaurs before. As she explained, she was amazed to discover that Medha had never even learned about extinction. Nancy vowed at that point that she would never allow herself to remain ignorant on any topic.

"There, Sister Peterman. Do you like it?"

Nancy was finished cutting the woman's hair. Sister Peterman looked at herself critically in the mirror and then shrugged. "I guess it's okay for a beauty school student."

Nancy felt the urge to quickly make just one more snip, one that would ruin the look of Sister Peterman's hair, but she wasn't stupid. Nancy's father was a high priest, and Brother Peterman was the High Priest group leader. No sense making things harder on her dad.

"What would you have liked differently?" asked Nancy carefully. "I'm always anxious to learn. And maybe there's something I can still do to make it better."

"No, no, it's fine. I'll be okay, I guess. I don't have to go out in public all that much these days."

Nancy gritted her teeth. "Well, you be sure to ask your doctor about prochlorperazine."

"Oh…yes, certainly."

"Can you say it? I know it's five syllables long. Americans aren't used to words with more than two or three syllables. When I taught myself Italian, though, I learned their word for 'camera' was 'macchina fotografica.' Eight syllables. So you ought to be able to manage five."

Sister Peterman turned an icy stare on Nancy. "Know-it-all," she muttered under her breath.

Nancy smiled sweetly and led her to the door. Then she swept the floor to get ready for her next client. Although still a student, she'd learned so much already that even the teacher was picking up tips from her. Nancy wasn't obnoxious about it, though. She'd say, "Do you think this would work?" and pretend to be tentative as she demonstrated a technique she was certain was good. The teacher would usually smile patronizingly, but then Nancy could see him using it to teach her classmates later.

It seemed to Nancy that knowledge was meant to be shared. She couldn't understand the proprietary attitude so many people had toward it. When her father was working on an experiment in his biology lab, he was so afraid someone would steal his ideas that he wouldn't even discuss them at home with his family. It seemed sad to Nancy that people had to live this way. Her dismay must have been the way Native Americans felt about the Europeans coming over and claiming to own the land. Land was something that belonged to everyone.

So was knowledge.

It was like the reports Nancy heard on the news. North Korea and Iran had to be prevented from learning how to make nuclear weapons. That knowledge was reserved for *good* people, like Americans. But whether or not Iranians were any better politically than the Chinese or Pakistani, as humans, they had a right to all the knowledge that any other humans were privy to.

Even the Church believed in a hierarchy of knowledge, though. The prophets and apostles were privileged to know certain things the rest of the sheep-like mass of saints weren't allowed to hear. If it was useful or relevant to salvation and exaltation, however, why couldn't they *all* know it?

Those who knew of Nancy's thirst for knowledge were a little surprised when she enrolled in a hairdressing course upon graduation from high school. She simply felt it was a way to make money on her own schedule while attending college, and she intended to go to college until she had earned at least three or four degrees.

Sister Walker knocked on her door. It was time for Nancy's next appointment. "How are you doing today?" asked Nancy with a smile.

"Oh, just wonderful. Just wonderful. My little Billy is getting smarter all the time. Do you know what he said the other day?"

"What?"

"'Your hair is dying. It's turning all black at the bottom.' Isn't that just adorable?" Sister Walker laughed.

"I hope you told him hair is already dead. Just like fingernails. They get longer, but they don't really 'grow.'"

Sister Walker looked at Nancy oddly. "No, I didn't tell him that."

They chatted about unimportant things as Nancy worked on Sister Walker's hair. The Church was good at community. When the Relief Society heard that Nancy was taking customers at home to learn how to do hair, half of the sisters had called her within two weeks to make appointments. After Sister Walker left, Nancy had just one more appointment today, with the Relief Society president herself, who arrived promptly on schedule. "If you're any good," Sister Whitcomb said with the hint of a smile, "I may let you work on my hair when I become a god."

Nancy looked at her with puzzlement, but Sister Whitcomb went on. "Wouldn't you like to be a hairdresser to the gods?"

"Does hair still grow after we're resurrected?" Nancy asked in confusion.

"Well, sure. You wouldn't want to be stuck with the same hairdo throughout eternity, would you? That would be hell, not heaven."

Nancy couldn't tell if Sister Whitcomb was serious or not, but it set Nancy to thinking. If bodies were perfect after the resurrection, why did Joseph Smith see an older man with Jesus in his First Vision? Wouldn't God the Father be permanently about 25 or whatever the optimal, perfect age must have been for a resurrected body? Wouldn't all resurrected beings be the same age?

And why would white hair have been perfect for Heavenly Father? Gray hair was a defect on Earth. Was that no longer the case after you died?

Then, too, did God and Jesus and Adam and Peter all have six-packs? Gods had better be sexy, Nancy thought, if she had to have sex with the same one for billions of years.

But sex brought up another question. Was an intact hymen the sign of a perfect body or of an imperfect one? Did the hymen of goddesses reform after every birth of a spirit child before the next Celestial pregnancy could begin? And godly ovaries brought up another issue. Surely, resurrected goddesses didn't undergo menstruation. That was a mortal condition, a curse for Eve. Did the spirit eggs of women gods only descend upon command then, when it was time for fertilization? Or did goddesses get pregnant so regularly in heaven that as soon as one spirit baby popped out, they started on their next child? Perhaps pregnancy was the natural state of female gods throughout eternity. Nancy wasn't sure she wanted a permanently distended stomach, even if resurrected skin didn't get stretch marks.

She wondered just how different a perfect body, pregnant or not, would be from her present one. There wasn't supposed to be any blood in a resurrected body. The Church always made a point of saying "flesh and bone," not "flesh and blood." Those people had something like antifreeze in their veins.

"Do you enjoy cutting hair?" asked Sister Whitcomb, shaking Nancy out of her reverie.

"Oh, yes, it's very soothing."

"You think you'll make it a career?"

"I don't know. I think it might get old after a while. I'd prefer a career where there was always something new to learn. Perhaps I'll be a paleobotanist. Or a geophysicist."

"Well, dear, there is a finite amount of knowledge in all fields."

"Even in something like medicine?"

"Of course. You have to be able to find interest in your field even after you know everything. Otherwise, you'll never be fit to be a god."

"What do you mean?"

"God knows everything, doesn't He?"

"Yes."

"He's known everything for tens of billions of years already. And he'll never learn another new thing in the next ten billion years, either. You have to find not learning to be satisfying or you'll never be happy as a god."

Nancy lowered her scissors and stared at the back of Sister Whitcomb's head. Her heart was pounding. She felt adrenalin rushing through her body. She'd just heard words which she could feel were about to change her life.

"But...but learning is what makes life exciting. It's what makes life fun. Meaningful."

"You've got to find joy in other things, or you're doomed to disappointment."

"But...but..."

Nancy clipped away in a daze, wondering what to do with this new information. Should she not go to college? Should she put off learning as long as possible, to stretch it out? Instead of learning ten new facts a day, maybe she should drag it out to two a year. And then after she died, to one new fact every thousand years. It might take 200 billion years at that rate before she ran out of things to learn.

But what happened after that? Even if she put off the inevitable conclusion to a hundred trillion years, eternity was *forever*. There would be another hundred trillion years with nothing else to learn.

Maybe knowing everything was exciting in and of itself.

But for trillions and trillions and gazillions and googatillions of years?

Nancy felt sick and finished Sister Whitcomb's hair as quickly as she could.

"That's just lovely, dear," said Sister Whitcomb. "If you can at least make it to ministering angel status, maybe I *will* let you do my hair in the Celestial Kingdom."

Nancy forced a smile. "Can I be a pedicurist to the gods, too?" she asked coolly. "I'd hate to have too narrow a specialty.

I assume toenails still grow on resurrected bodies as well? Or do gods have their own nail clippers?"

"Perhaps you should take up the harp, dear."

"Why is that?" Nancy's mind was still reeling from these new ideas, but soon she'd be alone and could pray about all she'd just learned.

"You know, so you'll be prepared to be an angel right from the start. In case you don't make it to the top."

"I feel a little queasy," said Nancy, putting her hand on her stomach. "I'd better get a prochlorperazine."

Sister Whitcomb's eyebrows lifted. Then she smiled knowingly. "Such a smart girl, aren't you?"

Nancy shooed Sister Whitcomb out the door. She gulped her pill down with a diet lemonade and sat in her salon chair as she stared at the snippets of dyed hair on the floor. She felt like Sisyphus, cutting hair that would just grow right back. And yet she wished she could have a Sisyphean brain, always relearning everything as if it were right for the first time. Maybe gods had a celestial form of senility so that their long-term memory was affected and learning could always be new.

Nancy shook her head. How could the prospect of perfect knowledge and godhood be depressing? Surely, something was wrong with her.

She stood up listlessly and went outside to bicycle over to the library so she could check out another DVD on haircutting. She didn't know everything just yet, at least. She still had a *few* good years ahead of her.

Nancy rummaged through the DVDs half-heartedly until she found one that modestly intrigued her. She trudged up to the circulation desk and handed it to the librarian.

"Did you like the last one you checked out?" the librarian asked cheerily.

Nancy nodded glumly. "I suppose."

"You know, if you go online and find other DVDs on the subject you think might be more helpful, you can give us a list, and we'll submit it to the acquisitions department. You can help everyone else learn what you think they ought to know." She smiled at Nancy conspiratorially. "Oh, the power!" She laughed.

Nancy felt as if she'd been struck. "I will," she managed to say. "I will."

She pedaled home furiously, smiling. The answer was so obvious. She could be a librarian to the gods, or at least to those on their way to godhood. There would be an unending supply of new gods throughout eternity, and as long as she could be a part of *their* learning process, even if she weren't learning herself, she could still experience the excitement of acquiring new knowledge. After all, that's what God was doing with her right now, wasn't it?

Nancy locked her bike in the apartment building basement and climbed up to her floor. She went inside, slid the new DVD into the player, and plopped down on her sofa, leaning forward to see the screen. Learning *was* fun, and now that she was no longer afraid of running out of the sensation of wonderment, she could enjoy it again.

Nancy was going to be a know-it-all. She'd be a celestial geophysicist, and a celestial librarian, and a hairdresser to the gods. She was going to know *everything*. And help others to learn everything, too. That's what being a god meant.

Nancy watched eagerly as the man on the video demonstrated a new technique she hadn't seen before. She replayed the scene two times and took a few notes. Then she went on to the next screen, sighing deeply in pleasure. She hugged herself happily, watching scissors cut away before her, hair falling off the large apron, and she smiled.

But then she thought of something else.

If gods were perfect, why did they need clothing? That was like saying something was wrong with their form. Or that gods couldn't control their thoughts amongst each other. Every other species lived without clothing. Was shame a mark of perfection? Were all the birds and cats and horses and bees and butterflies sinfully immodest? How could you be perfect if you needed something outside of yourself, like fabric, to exist?

Nancy's mind kept racing.

If male gods had more than one wife, dozens or perhaps hundreds of them, did that mean that women were inherently superior to men? That there were 60 or 70 or 80 female gods to every male who made it to godhood? If that wasn't the case, there would have to be a lot of leftover, unmarried male gods up there.

Somehow, the more Nancy thought about heaven, the less any of it made sense. What if she was using her brain too much, thinking too many thoughts? Maybe *that* would keep her from the Celestial Kingdom. How could you qualify for the highest degree of heaven without using your brain to its fullest, and what if using it disqualified you, too? What if human intelligence were the equivalent of the Tyrannosaurus rex's arms? Did one have to avoid using one's brain in order to believe?

Nancy continued watching the hairstylist on the screen, clipping away and chattering happily, both knowledgeable and ignorant. And as Nancy watched, wondering how much ignorance she would have to embrace to keep her faith alive, her smile slowly faded away.

Counting Nozzles

"**O**h, shoot! I forgot the nozzles!" I said, reaching for the door handle.

I quickly walked past the two pump islands in front of the Gulf station and counted. Four pumps and six nozzles. They'd get a three rating. Not bad, since the highest was five.

"Come on, Gray," Wanda said almost in a whine as I sat back down in the car. "You're getting slower on each one. I want to finish and get home."

I didn't tell her that if she'd parked in a better position I wouldn't have had to get out of the car again. But she did have a point. After a week and a half of surveying gas stations, I shouldn't be forgetting such obvious points. It had been a long day, though, and we had finished fourteen outlets before lunch and five since then. We were ahead of schedule and I didn't feel like killing myself just because Wanda needed to get home early to buy some fabric she'd forgotten to get the day before.

I picked up the portable computer and put it on my lap. Snapping open the cover, I called up the first panel and began entering in the information I had gathered. Fortunately, Wanda didn't talk when I was on the machine. She'd sing along with the radio or read the scriptures, but at least she didn't talk to me. Wanda was a nice enough woman at times, but she'd been griping all day. I had half the money for my ticket to Austria, though, so putting up with her was at least profitable.

The first three panels in the computer needed little correction, but I had to add in the new fuel prices and new hours that had changed since the survey done two years before. I also had to guess on the volume of gasoline pumped each month because the manager hadn't wanted to tell me for fear that we would use the information against him. I hoped my work wasn't going to be used to hurt people. I did get the job, after all, through the Church.

"One more thing," I said, hopping out of the car again. What was the matter with me today? I was forgetting everything. I checked the price for the car wash and then headed back.

"I thought you were through," said the attendant I'd talked with earlier.

"Almost." I smiled.

"Is that your wife in the car?" he asked. "I'd like to work with mine, too."

"Oh, no," I said, laughing. "Just friends." I shuddered as I walked back to the car. Wanda was just another member of my congregation, and much older than I was as well.

"All finished?" asked Wanda as I closed the computer a minute later. She put the car in reverse and began backing out.

"Yes," I said, a little irritated that she always left before I could look up the next address.

"I need to get that fabric today if I'm going to finish Sister Martin's wedding dress by Saturday, so we need to hurry."

I opened the plot map given me by the company and then compared it with a map of the Westbank. They had sent me to the one part of New Orleans I knew nothing about, but I was learning fast, having to visit all 179 gas outlets on this side of the river. "The next one is on the corner of Lapalco and Belle

Chasse." I folded the maps in half and put them back above the dashboard.

"I have to get a picture of this one first," said Wanda. She pulled out of the station and crossed Lapalco. Then she turned around, and as she approached the station again, she got out her Polaroid camera, stopped the car in the middle of the street, and took a picture. Then Wanda put the car in drive and we headed for the next station. "I hope this one has a bathroom," she said. "I'll be floating soon."

"Yeah."

"And I hope it's got toilet paper."

"You should have picked some up at my house this morning."

"I'm telling ya!" She laughed. "Who did that to your house?"

"I don't know yet." I did, though. It was my 15-year-old step-brother, Dean. Up until now, we'd gotten along well in the nine months that my Dad and his Mom had been married. We'd played basketball in the afternoon, not because I particularly liked the game but because I wanted to spend time with him. We also discussed the Middle East, homelessness, AIDS, gay rights, and anything else in the news. I remembered when I was his age, no one felt I was grown enough to talk about the news. But how old did you have to be to deserve being able to talk about life? Besides, I suspected Dean might be gay and need someone to talk to. I was gay myself though I certainly hadn't told him or anyone else about it. But I knew how to be supportive if Dean dropped any hints. I could encourage him to abstain and to go on a mission as I had. Then he'd be strong enough to stay in the Church and get married. I'd feel I'd accomplished something good in my life that might make up for my gayness. I certainly hadn't baptized many people in Austria. So whether or not we were friends because we could both sense the same thing in each other, or for whatever reason, we did seem to get along better than most step-siblings.

At church, though, Dean and I never let on that we got along because I was his Sunday School teacher, and it wouldn't have been cool for his friends to know he liked the teacher. But at home, we even planned together a six-month anniversary party for our parents. Then last week my Dad finally insisted on a separation after having considered it for three months. Louise started looking for an apartment right away, and Dean left immediately to stay with friends. He hadn't spoken to me since, as if the break up were somehow my fault.

I worried that the separation would drive him away from the Church, that he'd hate the Church as well as us. I knew Dean was sometimes spiteful, having TP'ed the homes of some classmates at school he didn't like, but I'd still been surprised to see the rolls of white toilet paper all over our yard this morning. I was sure he'd done it.

"How did your kids react to your divorce, Wanda?" I asked suddenly. No one knew of the separation yet, so I hoped she wouldn't grow suspicious. My Dad didn't want to broadcast his private life, but I suspected Louise was already beginning to spread the news of how she had been "kicked out of the house."

"Oh, pretty well," she replied. "Rob was such a jerk we were all glad to be rid of him. He wasn't even a member of the Church, you know. He wasted all his money on gambling. I just couldn't take it any more. The only problem the kids had was when I remarried and they had to start taking orders from a man they'd never seen before. I guess you know what it's like having a step-parent."

Unfortunately. Although I'd gotten along well enough with Dean, I always had to hide my true feelings about his mother. After my Mom had died in a car accident three years ago, I had expected my father to marry again. After all, he was only forty-five. But when he brought Louise home last October and announced a day later that they were engaged, I was shocked. I'd hoped at least to get a chance to know her first, but even my Dad didn't get that chance. Nine weeks after he met her, they were married. She moved in and threw out half of my Mom's things while I was at school one day, without even offering to let me have any of them. Then she changed the drapes, the carpet, rearranged the furniture, changed everything around in the kitchen, and made me feel like an outcast in my own home I'd lived in all my life. She even wanted to rearrange my room, and hinted almost every day when my father wasn't around that I was old enough to move out and should do so. That last may have been true, of course, but was really between my father and me. He'd told me I could stay at home until I graduated from college, and that was still one semester away.

"They all get along fine now," continued Wanda. "How about you and Louise?"

"Oh, fine," I answered. Really, though, she always managed to find something wrong with the way I dressed, or the way I washed the dishes, or the way I did anything. "You'll like this," she'd say, placing a dessert on the table. "It has a lot of sugar." I was all of five pounds overweight. Or she'd ask me to help clean the garage of one of her friends, on the day she knew I was going to the library to work on a paper. "Oh, I guess not," she'd say as if to herself, before giving me a chance to reply. "That would require work, wouldn't it?"

She'd even say things like that to my Dad. "Oh, you'll like this movie, dear. It doesn't require any thought." Then she'd laugh to pretend she was joking. I was impressed that my high school graduate father hadn't been intimidated by marrying a woman with a PhD, but I did wonder why she had married him. She'd quit work immediately, saying she finally had a chance to be a full-time mother as the Church encouraged. I certainly didn't notice her spending lots of time on Dean, though. She seemed to prefer planning parties, complaining that my Dad wasn't very sociable when he quickly grew tired of them.

I was glad that my Mom and Dad had always gotten along well. They'd been married for twenty-six years, and I never heard them so much as raise their voices to each other. Mom went to Dad's tractor pulls to support him, though they bored her out of her mind, and he took her on a date once a week, usually out to eat, which my father felt was an extravagance but which my Mom loved. Once every couple of months, Dad would take her to a movie, though only twice in my life had I ever heard him say he actually enjoyed a movie. The first was *True Grit* and the second *Foul Play*. But he patiently sat through every Elvis Presley movie ever made. What he preferred, and what my Mom liked as well, was to take off to the Smokey Mountains for a few days. I never heard them say they loved each other, but there was an awful lot to be said simply for the absence of bickering. It was nice to see that a good marriage was at least possible. It would probably get a four rating, I thought, smiling as I glanced down at my computer. It made me believe that a five could be achieved with a little more work, and maybe a little luck.

"I guess Brother and Sister Martin are glad to be going to the temple," I said. "How long have they been members now?"

"Over a year," Wanda replied. "I think a temple marriage is so much nicer than a normal one. I don't even like to think of my marriage to Rob. Of course, my wedding to Michael was probably nicer because I didn't have morning sickness at the time." She laughed.

"Probably so."

"Is that it?" asked Wanda then, pointing off to the right.

"Yeah." I quickly scribbled down all the information I could as we approached the outlet. A Time Saver. Supplied by Amoco. Good. That meant a contract dealer, and it was one question less I'd have to ask in my interview. Two curb cuts on the primary street. Prices posted. Hours posted. Convenience food, of course. And yes, they had electronic pumps. I got out of the car, checked off the number of pumps and nozzles, and walked into the store.

As I waited in line behind the other customers, I noticed a *Star* newspaper near the check-out. "Liz to Marry Eighth Time!" "Madonna's Secret Lovers!" Oh, please. Didn't people have anything more important to concern themselves with than worrying about other people's love lives?

Three more people got in line, so I stepped out and went to the back of the last person because we weren't supposed to make the employees mad by disturbing their paying customers. I smiled, knowing Wanda was probably already getting impatient. I'd been acquainted with her for eight years, and she was certainly a lot nicer now than she used to be before her divorce. This was the first time I'd ever worked with her directly, though. She was on Church welfare, so the Bishop had helped her get this two-week job. I was saving up to go to Austria to get married, so the Bishop told me about the job as well. In return, I donated two days labor at the Bishop's storehouse in Slidell, filling food orders for poorer members of the Church who needed help. I wasn't required to work at the storehouse, but it was fun, and I felt I ought to give as well as take. Kind of like my Mom and Dad did in their marriage.

I knew that in my own marriage, it would probably be harder. When Wiltrude had come to visit for two months last year, I had planned to take her on a swamp tour, wanting her to get a feel for my home. She'd refused, saying she was afraid she'd see a snake, and she'd been mad when I asked if I could go alone, telling her it was something I'd long wanted to do, and my Dad's friend offering the free tour might not offer again. I was mystified that she would be upset over this, but she said we only had two months together and shouldn't spend it being apart. She was usually so reasonable that her anger worried me for what it might mean for the future. Was it really possible to get along always with anyone, even someone you liked?

I sighed as the line moved ahead slowly. The man at the counter now was buying a six-pack of Coors. I wondered if his wife minded his drinking. Or was the beer for her and not for him? I remembered when Louise left, she took me aside and said, "I know this is hard for you, but you need to know that the reason your father is kicking me out is because he's an alcoholic and I've been trying to get him into rehabilitation." I tried to look serious so she'd feel she scored a point, but all I could think was that Dad had never missed a day at work, and he always looked sober at home. We'd been Mormons for thirteen years, and he'd never drunk even before we joined the Church.

There were two beers in the fridge after Louise left, but they were still sitting there. I was sure she'd put them there in the first place, to worry me, which it did, slightly. If I could have a secret like being gay, my Dad could have one like being

161

an alcoholic. But every day when I looked in the fridge, the two beers were still there.

When I went home today, I expected I'd still find them in the fridge. I hoped I'd also find when I got home a reply from one of the schools in Austria to which I'd sent job applications. I would be graduating from the University of New Orleans in a few months and hoped to be able to teach English in Austria. Wiltrude's parents weren't pleased at first with the idea of her marrying a foreigner, but when they discovered two months ago that Wiltrude's sister was dating an Ethiopian member in Vienna, she said I suddenly looked a lot better to them, though they were slowly adapting to her sister's choice as well.

I couldn't help but wonder if Wiltrude and I would be able to stay together. We were going to be married in the Mormon temple in Bern, Switzerland. Marriages in temples weren't "till death do you part," but were to last for all eternity. But Dad and Louise had been married in the Atlanta temple, hadn't they?

Another man stepped in line behind me. Forget it. The interview wasn't that important. My supervisor had told me not to waste too much time if I couldn't get any information. There had to be priorities in this work. I'd guess at what I didn't know. I stepped out of the line and walked back to the car.

"Good interview?" asked Wanda when I was in my seat again.

"Didn't find out anything."

"After all this time?" She sighed in frustration. "Shit!"

I smiled, thinking again of Wiltrude. No matter how surprised she was by something or how maddening someone might be, she never even said "Mist!" or "Verflixt!" equivalent to our "darn" and "drat." She certainly never said

162

"scheißdreck." She said she felt she should be in control of her emotions. One of the first things I'd observed about her was her sincere smile when faced with rejection by other people, which happened to us hourly as missionaries. I'd seen her calmly wipe the saliva off her face after a woman had spit on her. She'd then gone over to a Schreibwarenladen, bought a card, gone a few doors down to a shop to buy stamps, and mailed the card to herself. Then she'd resumed her work.

I'd also noticed how she refused to talk negatively about one of her companions who we both knew had taken advantage of her. That was when I decided I needed to get to know her better. If she wouldn't criticize these people I felt she had every right to be angry with, maybe she wouldn't get too mad at me if I accidentally offended her. But it was curious that when I finally began considering marrying her, it was with the thought, "Well, if I *have* to get married..." Surely, she deserved better than that.

But I *did* have to get married. It was a commandment of God. Without a marriage, a successful marriage at that, I couldn't get to the highest degree of heaven to live with God. Even if I managed to be celibate, something praised by some other religions, as a Mormon I'd be condemned to a lower degree of heaven, which in essence was still hell since I'd be denied further progression. And if I didn't marry, I knew I'd never be strong enough to be celibate. God only knew what kind of depravity I would fall into then. Even now at school, I found myself watching the other male students, almost praying one would approach me. I needed a wife to protect me, but I also needed a wife I knew I could live with.

Fortunately, Wiltrude and I had been able to work together for over seven months, three in Graz and four in Vienna. Then a year after our missions were over, we'd spent another three weeks together in Salzburg, where I'd given her my mother's engagement ring on the banks of the Salzach River, and then a week more in her home town of Innsbruck in the west, where she gave me a silver "promise" ring as we stood on her parents' balcony.

During her two-month visit to New Orleans the following year, she stayed in the room across the hall from mine. We lay on the sofa together to watch T.V., and I did enjoy feeling her warmth against me. We'd French kissed three times, and I'd even managed to get an erection once, which was promising. It had been over a year since I had seen her now, and I was looking forward to getting back over there.

Our long distance romance was convenient in that I'd had a full-fledged relationship for years now with only a couple of hours invested each week. In some ways, it seemed better than marriage itself. But we did need kids, and maybe sex with a woman, as unsatisfying as it was sure to be, would still be enough to keep me from thinking of men too much. I had decided right from the beginning that I couldn't let Wiltrude know I was gay. I was afraid she'd feel unloved if she knew, and I didn't want that. Besides, it wasn't as if I'd ever actually had sex with another man. I was still a virgin, after all.

Opening my computer, I entered all the new information I'd managed to collect even with my wandering thoughts, and I guessed at the rest. "How many nozzles did you count?" asked Wanda. Then she giggled. "God. The number of nozzles I've counted in my life. Michael makes how many?" She looked at me and laughed. "You have to be careful," she said. "You can't just pull up to a pump and pick any nozzle. You have to get one with the right kind of gas." She squealed and hit the dashboard. Then she picked up her scriptures while I continued on my computer.

The machine buzzed at me once for a mistake I'd made in saying liter instead of gallon, and I quickly corrected my entry. An hour later, we'd finished three more outlets. It was only 3:15, a half hour before we were supposed to stop for the day, but Wanda insisted we head back to base. We were silent as we crossed the Mississippi River. Then there was some traffic on the high rise over the Industrial Canal, but before too long, we were at the La Quinta in New Orleans East, and after a brief explanation to my supervisor about why we'd come in early, I turned in my computer and maps and picked up two more packets of film and a handful of new survey sheets.

Then I was back in the car and Wanda was driving me home. She only lived a mile away from me in Kenner, and I was right on her way, so she picked me up and dropped me off every day. It saved me a tank or two of gas, and she was being paid for her mileage whereas I wouldn't be, since she was "the driver," so it worked out fine for both of us, though I still recognized it as a favor and appreciated it.

"Hope you get your fabric before the store closes," I said.

"Oh, I'll be there by 4:30, so I'll make it," she replied. "Then I'll sew all evening. What are you going to do?"

"The Single Adults are playing volleyball tonight."

"Sounds like fun."

"If Lynn remembers to bring her ball." I smiled, thinking of our sometimes disorganized meetings, and the disorganized people I had to work with. I hadn't expected the call to be in charge of all the Mormon Singles in the New Orleans area two years ago. The call had come from the Bishop right after I'd announced my engagement and didn't consider myself single anymore. Was he saying he didn't like my choice of Wiltrude?

Or did he want me to be an example in showing everyone that getting married was better than staying single?

I'd heard some of the other singles say things like, "I'll be so happy when I finally get married," or "I'll sure be happy when I finish school," and other things like this, but it seemed to me that we shouldn't put off being happy, that it was far too fleeting an emotion to risk postponing to any degree. If we couldn't be satisfied with ourselves now while we were alone, I didn't see how we could really expect to be happy later, either. Instead, my thought was often, "I'm reasonably happy now, everything considered. I sure hope I'll still be as happy when I get married." All I knew was that my every "date" for the past couple of years consisted in ten minutes of reading Wiltrude's letter and an hour or so in writing mine to her, and I had not felt terribly deprived of her company. I instead enjoyed reading and listening to music and taking walks and playing Scrabble and talking with friends. I enjoyed going wherever I wanted and staying as long as I liked.

I remembered in Vienna my companion, Elder Hof, and I had gone to visit a church member one evening for just a few minutes. But Elder Hof had gotten caught up in the conversation, and even by 10:00, he wasn't ready to leave. The mission rule was bedtime at 10:30, so at 10:15, I suggested again that we leave. Even though I was senior companion, Elder Hof shrugged me off and kept talking. At 10:30, he still wasn't ready. At 10:50, I stood up and walked to the door. It took him another five minutes to decide to follow me. We didn't say a word all the way home. The fact was, however, that this guy had been my favorite companion of them all. There wouldn't have been a problem even that night except that we were a "couple," and I couldn't leave when I wanted and just say, "See you tomorrow." The "couple" part put an awful lot of extra strain on our relationship, always having to decide on *everything* together.

And yet always having Elder Hof with me had been comforting as well. I never had to face any boring meeting, and creepy mission leader, any rude person alone. We shared the experience of getting chased down a stairwell by a man with a handgun. Rather than feel freaked out by the experience, as I may well have done if I was alone, we'd laughed when we reached safety. We shared the experience of peeing together off the roof of a nine-story building. It wasn't a glorious experience, to be sure, but there was a certain intimacy involved that didn't happen in just a regular friendship. And we shared the experience of teaching a young couple only a few years older than us about the Church, and we baptized the couple together. It did mean more to me because I did it with a companion I really liked.

I had looked on every companion as a marriage partner, trying to see if I could make our relationship work, thinking of the days when marriages had been arranged by others. As my mission progressed, I'd count them off, finding that I'd been able to survive all of them. Every time now in church when I was called to work closely with someone, I viewed the relationship as a trial marriage to see if I could make it. I'd survived all of these as well, but I wanted more than survival out of marriage. I'd had true success with Elder Hof, someone just thrust upon me by an arbitrary decision of our mission president. Surely, by choosing my own partner, I could make an even better success. Especially if that person had also had the experience of having missionary companions.

"I met my husband Michael at a Single Adults meeting," said Wanda, bringing me back. "We were married three months later. Which reminds me. Heard from your girlfriend recently?"

"Last Saturday."

"Y'all set a date yet?"

"Well, we've set the year."

Wanda laughed. "You better not put it off much longer. How old are you now, anyway?"

"Twenty-four." I decided against telling her that Wiltrude was three and a half years older than I was.

"I really don't approve of missionaries looking for a wife while they're on missions, but—"

"I wasn't looking," I replied, sighing, having heard this already from several other people. "I simply found her."

"But how can you get to know her without dating?" she persisted. "Y'all must have done more than you should have."

I laughed. I hadn't even masturbated more than a handful of times out there, even that being considered a serious sin. "We were just good friends on our missions. Isn't that what the basis of a relationship should be?"

Wanda was silent for a moment. Then she said, "But being in love is different. You need to be in love to get married."

"I don't know," I said. "I counseled several couples when I was a missionary. We weren't really supposed to, but sometimes when we were knocking on doors, people would just pull us in and start telling us all their problems. Most of them would mention how the 'magic' was gone and now there was nothing left."

"But it doesn't have to go away," Wanda insisted. "It'll stay if it's the right person. And if you don't have it at the beginning, then you *know* it's not right."

I considered for a moment and then shook my head. I masturbated all too frequently these days, always thinking of men, often of one incredibly attractive blond missionary serving in my congregation, though I felt rather proud that I'd managed never to fantasize about Elder Hof, even if I did occasionally still have wet dreams about him. Sometimes when I masturbated, I'd pull out a picture of Wiltrude at the last second, trying to make an association between orgasm and her, but the trick usually left me feeling sick in addition to the guilt I usually experienced when just thinking of men.

"If being in love means swooning," I said, "or not being able to sleep because I keep thinking of her or not being able to be happy now while we're apart, then I guess I'm not in love." And I hoped I never would be. After we were transferred away from each other, Elder Hof had been deeply depressed, writing me many letters saying how much he missed me, but because I was so afraid of falling in love with him, I'd *refused* to feel bad after he was gone. I didn't want anyone, even a man, to have that kind of control over me. Because if anyone did ever have that kind of control, it would be a man, and I'd definitely be in trouble.

"Well, then why—"

"But I can't think of another person that I care for more deeply and want to spend my life with. She's my best friend, I miss being with her, and I'm glad we'll be back together again soon." And it was mostly true. Though I was happy enough, I really had no close friends here, and I was afraid of becoming too content with what the Church said was only half a life. There was a lot to be said for being single, but the longer I stayed unmarried, the more likely I was to become set in my ways and be unable to change or adapt as I needed to. I knew I couldn't make Wiltrude wait any longer than she already was without having to worry about losing her. I only hoped I could stop wishing for nozzles and could be content with just the gas tank.

Wanda made a little noise in her throat but didn't say anything else. We both listened to the radio while we drove for another fifteen minutes to get to our exit. As we turned down West Esplanade and headed for my home, I wondered what I'd find. Had Louise taken more of her things off to her new apartment? When she and my Dad had argued in the last few months, she'd push him in the chest and scream, "Hit me! Hit me!" right in his face. I knew she'd worked with the Battered Women's Program before marrying my Dad. It seemed to me that someone who could be as sick and devious as to try to provoke a violent crime was capable of almost anything. My Dad would always just walk out of the house then, leaving Louise fuming. I wondered that if she'd come to get her things, if she'd taken some of ours, too. I stared at the canal alongside the road and let my mind go blank.

Wanda stopped in front of my house a few minutes later, dropped me off, and then waved as she continued on. I looked at our green lawn I'd mowed yesterday. It looked fresh and cool. The toilet paper was all gone. I walked to the back door and unlocked it, closing my eyes and breathing deeply. Maybe my letter from Austria had come today. I stepped inside and closed the door behind me.

Shark among the Whales

Miranda hurriedly packed her suitcase. The mayor had just announced a mandatory evacuation for New Orleans, stating that the hurricane bearing down on the city was "the mother of all storms." After that last horrible hurricane, Miranda wasn't taking any chances. She laid her most expensive clothes on the bottom of the suitcase. She could never afford to replace them. And then she put all her scrubs on top, in case the city was destroyed and she had to get a job somewhere else.

Miranda's car wouldn't make it to Baton Rouge in ten hours of stop and go traffic, so she drove to the parish office building on Clearview. There she joined huge throngs of people, mostly black, and waited for a bus. She could tell the blacks were wondering what a white girl was doing evacuating with them.

"She looks rich," she heard one of them say. "What's she doing here?"

Of course, Miranda wasn't rich. She'd lost three jobs in the past year and a half, and she had unpaid payday loans out with three different companies. If only everyone at work wasn't so mean. She'd lost her last job at the end of probation, because they found out she had a lawsuit pending at her job before that. They'd technically fired her at that other hospital for moving some cookies a patient's family had donated to the nurse's station, but she knew it was really because of the head lice.

Still, she didn't think she could sue based on medical discrimination. She sued because they had called her a slut. A slut! And she hadn't had sex in ten years!

Miranda was 47 now. She'd had a hysterectomy two years earlier and now would never have children. It had been a huge blow, but just as big a blow had been when Keith had died of Lou Gehrig's disease. He'd been married to his second wife for twelve years by then, but Miranda had always believed he'd come back to her. Even when he was limping on his cane, hardly able to walk, he'd come over and try to rip her clothes off. She'd insist they get married first, but he'd just laugh and masturbate while looking at her. She knew he really loved her.

But Keith was dead now and she was alone.

Miranda climbed aboard a bus with some other poor people, hoping her suitcase wouldn't get lost or stolen. A fat black man sat next to her, resting his hand halfway on her leg. But she was a little hefty herself and couldn't squeeze herself over any further into her seat.

Twenty-four hours on the bus. It was going to be hell.

But it wasn't twenty-four hours. They drove to the airport instead. They were going to fly the evacuees somewhere. Oh god, thought Miranda. Please, not Salt Lake City. What would she do among all those Mormons?

She remembered the Mormon doctor from the hospital. He'd been nice to her until the hysterectomy, when Miranda had been forced to go to church for the first time in twenty years, to get welfare money from the bishop until she was back on her feet.

Miranda had been sitting in the back of the chapel one day, crying softly over her loss, when she distinctly heard the bishop's wife whisper to the doctor's wife next to her, "The Lord didn't want someone like that having children." The doctor had been cool to her ever since.

But the police wouldn't tell the evacuees where they were going. They just herded the mass of people along. At security, the guards looked through her luggage, and when they saw the nice clothes on the bottom, one of them said, "She's just in this for the FEMA money."

But that wasn't the worst. She heard a police officer tell a Red Cross worker standing next to the line, "Be careful. She's got head lice."

That proved the police were stalking her. As if she needed any more proof. One of the nurses who hated her, two hospitals ago, had been dating a police officer, and ever since, Miranda had seen police cruisers circling her apartment building, and overheard them talking about her when she ran into them in convenience stores. "That's the girl," she heard one of them say once as she walked past them near a casino on the lakefront. "That's the home wrecker."

It just made her so mad. She hadn't actually dated either the Arab doctor or the Jewish one. She'd just been nice to them both because they'd been nice to her. Was that so wrong? She wasn't trying to break up their families. It would have been different if they'd decided to divorce on their own and then start dating her. But she was no home wrecker!

Once on the plane, Miranda found herself sitting next to another fat black man. He kept leaning over onto Miranda, pretending he simply wanted to see out the window, but Miranda wasn't fooled. She knew what was going on. But there was nothing she could do. Maybe she should tell him she had head lice. People said blacks didn't get lice, but she knew they did.

"Okay, folks, now that we're in the air, we can tell you you're on your way to Louisville, Kentucky."

There was a mixed rumbling of both approval and disapproval. Miranda didn't really care where she went, as long as it was far away. She'd brought her resume' with her. If Louisville looked okay, she might just look for a job there and get a fresh start. Hospitals were so incestuous in New Orleans. Every time she was driven from one place to another, someone at the new hospital would have a friend from the other and the rumors would transfer along with her.

As New Orleans faded away behind her, Miranda realized she was like Lehi in the Book of Mormon, having left her homeland to escape the impending destruction coming to punish the unrepentant sinners, like those nurses who stayed behind. The other evacuees with her, though, were like Laman and Lemuel, unbelievers who had been forced out with the good but who would bring a terrible storm sometime later along the voyage.

A few hours later, they were at the Louisville airport, and as the bus took her to the convention center, she noticed how clean the city looked, very different from New Orleans. Soon she was set up on a cot along with 2000 other people, almost all of them black. A cute guy in dreadlocks started putting his things on the cot next to Miranda, but a Red Cross worker came over and told him, "We're trying to keep the single men separated from the single women."

The man rolled his eyes and looked at Miranda with a smile. She smiled back, just to be nice, but then she overheard the Red Cross worker whisper, "She has head lice," and the man picked up his things and moved away.

Miranda didn't care. She didn't like men with dreadlocks, anyway. She sat on her cot for a while but then began feeling antsy, so she got up to walk around. On the far end of the room, she heard two women arguing. She was going to steer around the fracas, but as she got closer, she could overhear that the women were arguing about religion. Then, to her amazement, she realized it was a Mormon woman arguing with a Jehovah's Witness.

Miranda wasn't at all sure she still believed in the Church, but it was exciting seeing someone else who did. Maybe it would be like in the Book of Mormon when Ammon and the Lamanite king fell down prostrate, and Miranda could go around like the secret Lamanite convert woman Abish and gather everyone together and have them all witness a miracle.

The Church always looked down on her. But she might bring a thousand converts to baptism now. Men in the Church would start wanting to be around her again. Miranda watched the argument progress, her heart pounding as she waited for them to be overcome by the power of the Spirit. The hurricane was simply God's way of bringing all these other people together to see this. Miranda was going to be famous in the Church. And she was going to have a prominent Mormon husband.

The Jehovah's Witness snapped her Bible shut in the Mormon woman's face, and Miranda could see the Mormon woman was livid. Cut her, cut her, Miranda urged the woman in her mind. Make her need a transfusion and then let God heal her.

But the Mormon woman just turned on her heels and walked off.

Just like a Mormon, thought Miranda in disgust. Always wimps. That's why they didn't like her. Because she stood up for herself. Mormons didn't approve of strong women like she was.

But they'd like her when she had money, when she won her lawsuit. They'd want her tithing. She smiled as she thought about the bishop being nice to her for a change. She'd make the bishop's wife be nice to her, too.

Miranda was exhausted after a twelve-hour shift at work followed by staying up listening to the news reports and then packing and flying. It was still early, but she lay down on her cot and went right to sleep.

In the middle of the night, though, she heard a woman one cot over yelling. "I can't breathe! I can't breathe!"

She sure had a lot of lung power for someone with no breath, thought Miranda. A Red Cross worker came over and gave the woman some nose spray, and things settled down again.

The next morning, breakfast was served, and Miranda wolfed it down. She'd missed dinner the night before. Of course, she could stand to lose forty pounds, so it was no great loss. But now her hair was a mess, and she had no make-up. She must look a horror.

"Is there anything you need?" a Red Cross worker asked her, moving from person to person.

"I could use a blow dryer," Miranda said. The people near her snickered.

Some buses came shortly after breakfast and took everyone to the amusement park, where they were given free admission. But rides always made Miranda feel sick, so she just walked around and looked at everything. It was too hard to really enjoy her "vacation," though, knowing she wasn't getting paid for these days off. Sitting on a bench enjoying the breeze, she overheard two black people talking next to her. "Look at her posing, trying to get a man." Miranda stood up and walked away.

The next day, Miranda discovered that the Red Cross had divided everyone into groups. Miranda laughed when she heard the names. There were the whales, and sure enough, the group consisted of people who just lay around on their cots all day. Then there were the parrots, the people who kept talking and talking all day and half the night. There were also the antelopes, the people who ran around and played ball all day. But Miranda was upset to discover she had been grouped with the sharks. These were the anti-social people who just wandered around on their own and only showed up for meals. She was a little put out by the label, but she realized she didn't want to belong to any of the other categories, either. Why couldn't there be a group of butterflies? Or hummingbirds? Or something else nice?

Today, everyone who wanted to go was bused to the Mohamed Ali museum. The blacks loved it, and Miranda had to admit, it was pretty impressive.

Back at the convention center, she learned that the hurricane had missed New Orleans and struck central Louisiana, but there was still some damage in the city, some power outages, and people weren't allowed to return just yet.

While she was eating dinner, Miranda heard two of the Red Cross workers talking about her. "Look how much she eats!"

Why would they say such a thing? Miranda fumed as she walked back to her cot. It wasn't as if she served herself. She was given a plate like everyone else, with no more food and no less on her plate than on any other. Why were people always so mean to her?

177

That night around 3:00, Miranda woke up when the woman beside her began yelling. "I need a glass of water! I need a glass of water!"

The woman wasn't a cripple. Why didn't she just get up and get some water herself? Sheesh.

In the morning, Miranda took a shower. The Red Cross had set up some good showers, but there were several women who didn't want to use them, choosing instead to bathe in the sinks where everyone had to brush their teeth. And they bathed their feces-covered babies there, too. There was always hair left all over the sinks and counters. It was repulsive.

But today, the group was given free admission to the science museum. The place was mostly geared toward children, but it was still pretty interesting.

Miranda was getting bored, though. She wished she could go back to work, even if the other nurses made her life hell. She was only a nursing secretary, since she'd flunked out of nursing school, but the nurses always seemed to feel she was a threat anyway. When a cute doctor had come up to talk to her once, one of the nurses deliberately blocked his path and told him, "She's nothing but trouble. Stay away from her."

Miranda knew the nurses were afraid she'd marry a doctor. The doctors liked her because she was smart and funny and efficient. And really, despite the weight, she had a pretty face and a pretty voice, and she could tell more men looked at her breasts than at her pudgy stomach.

The Arab doctor had even invited her on a riverboat cruise, but one of the nurses overheard, and Miranda saw her run off to tell the other nurses. The next day, "mysteriously," the doctor changed his mind and invited a woman doctor instead. Miranda wasn't stupid, though. She knew the nurses had turned him against her.

The woman doctor was also Arabic, and she lived in Miranda's apartment complex. And one day when Miranda went to get her mail, she overheard two of her neighbors talking. "*She* thinks she can get *him*? Not with those pictures going around."

The apartment complex had just done major remodeling on everyone's apartment, enclosing the outdoor balconies into sunrooms. Miranda had suspected the workers might have installed spy cameras in her apartment and now she knew. There were pictures of her floating around on the internet! She already knew the police had tapped her phone. She could hear the clicks when she picked it up. But she obviously couldn't go to the police about any of this, so she went to the FBI.

She told her story, and the agent sounded sympathetic, but when he took her driver's license to make a copy, he gasped, though he tried to cover it up by faking a cough. And the very next day at Wal-Mart, Miranda saw one of the women she'd seen in the FBI office. She got close enough to overhear her talking on her cell phone. "Anyone who looks like that is a loser!" she heard the woman say. So the FBI wasn't going to help her because she took a bad drivers license picture!

Miranda had felt distraught. There simply had to be some justice in the world. The Church claimed to be the repository of truth and righteousness, so she went back to church and talked to the Mormon doctor she'd worked with before.

"You need to drop the lawsuit," he told her. "No one likes a troublemaker. No one is even going to hire you again."

"I won't need them to. This is a multi-million dollar lawsuit. It's sexual harassment."

"I'd be careful if I were you. You're stressing yourself out too much. You know, one of our members just committed suicide a couple of weeks ago. She drowned herself. She was found dead in her car."

Miranda was floored. He was actually threatening her life. He knew she walked along the lake every day for exercise. He was threatening that she'd be found dead one day. He was obviously hinting pretty openly, too. How could someone drown herself and then walk back to her car? Was the Church after her money? Did they think she was going to win the lawsuit? Was that what this was all about?

Miranda needed to find a job here in Louisville, get a brand new start. Of course, she thought every time she moved to a new hospital in New Orleans it would be a brand new start. And what if another nurse from back home had evacuated to Louisville, too? What if she was getting a job here as well? Oh, my god. Could she never get away from those horrible, horrible people? It wasn't fair.

That evening, she saw that the storm had moved into Arkansas and was causing flooding there. She hoped she could get back home soon. She was going to win that lawsuit and move far, far away.

Miranda felt restless, so she took another stroll around the auditorium. There were a few Hispanics, a few really white trash people, no Asians, and hordes of blacks. Almost everyone looked pretty uneducated, and missing teeth seemed to be a common theme. Most people came in family groups, it appeared, but one old black woman was sitting alone knitting. She'd evacuated with her knitting needles.

Miranda smiled and debated over whether or not to talk to the woman. She remembered the passage, "Wherefore ye have done it unto one of the least of these my brethren, ye have done it unto me." It was a sexist scripture, of course. Did it only count if you were nice to poor men, "brethren," and not women? Men always seemed to get the real breaks in life. Women fought each other over the scraps.

So Miranda walked up to the woman. "What are you knitting?" she asked softly.

"Baby blankets," the woman replied, not looking up. "I donate them to Goodwill."

"How sweet."

"You need to think of others first."

Miranda frowned. What did the woman mean by that? Had someone told her about the lawsuit? Did she think Miranda was being selfish to sue? What did that old woman know? She'd never been abused as Miranda had.

"Do *you* always think of others?" Miranda asked a little coldly.

"When you're all alone in the world, there's nothing else you can do, is there?"

And what did the woman mean by *that*? How did she know Miranda had no family? She was being awfully cheeky.

But she'd make one more attempt to be Christ-like. "Do you have a favorite color you like to knit?"

"All the colors of the rainbow. We need to remember God's promise after the Flood, especially in times like these. We can't forget God's goodness, no matter what happens." The woman gave Miranda a sharp look, and Miranda's mouth fell open.

Had someone told her about Miranda's miscarriage? How dare she accuse Miranda of forgetting about God? You tried to be nice to people and this was what you always got. Miranda turned around and walked off without a word.

The parrots and antelope kept her awake until late in the evening, but Miranda eventually fell asleep. In the middle of the night, though, the woman in the cot next to her began yelling again. "I have to pee! I have to pee!"

Miranda had had just about enough. She sat up and looked at the woman coldly. "I guess we'll have to get you a wheelchair if you can't get up and walk to the bathroom."

The woman shut up immediately. "I ain't going to no hospital!" She climbed out of the cot and walked off to the bathroom.

Miranda expected her neighbors would appreciate what she'd done, but she could hear one of them muttering, "What has she got against old black people?"

Miranda got up and walked toward her, but the woman started coughing. She did this every time Miranda got near her. Miranda knew the woman was simply trying to keep her away so she wouldn't catch her lice, but Miranda just fumed. What was worse? Getting head lice or getting tuberculosis? The woman had no reason to be so self-righteous.

Miranda took a walk around the auditorium. She stopped when she came upon the man with the dreadlocks. It would have been nice to have someone to talk to here.

A little girl was playing with a rubber ball, and Miranda watched her bounce it up and down. If she hadn't had that miscarriage…wait a minute. That was over 25 years ago. She could have a *granddaughter* this age by now. Miranda had always felt so maternal around children, but she didn't know what she should be feeling now. She certainly didn't want to feel grandmotherly. If she won the lawsuit, she'd have enough money to adopt a child. Maybe two. She'd still get her time as a mother. She wouldn't be cheated forever. Life was still going to be good for her.

The girl dropped her ball, and it rolled under a cot where a skinny man with track marks on his arms was sleeping. The girl looked as if she wanted her ball but was too afraid to retrieve it.

Miranda smiled at her and got down on the floor and reached under the cot. A police officer started walking toward her, but Miranda stood up and offered the ball to the girl, who turned and ran away.

Miranda walked back to her cot and went back to sleep.

The next day, everyone was bused to Churchill Downs. Miranda had never been much of a gambler. She only bought lottery tickets a few times a year. She wasn't about to waste her time fantasizing about impossible dreams. The Church said gambling was a sin. But it was interesting to see the place. She tried to memorize every detail so she could tell the Mormon doctor next time she saw him. She knew he'd disapprove, and that would be fun to watch. He'd be afraid she was going to lose all her money from the lawsuit, and the Church wouldn't get its cut. She smiled.

When she turned, she saw a TV camera in her face. Reporters had been following the evacuees around for days, showing everyone how nice the townspeople were being to them. Miranda had avoided being filmed, still upset about her hair. Her eyes grew big now and she twisted about and hurried off. What if the EEOC back in New Orleans saw her looking like this? They'd drop her case. Had the hospital paid the reporters to follow her? She knew they'd paid off some of the doctors to testify against her. She'd overheard the charge nurse talking about it.

The nurses had also said she was white trash, that when they saw her shopping on her days off, she was dressed too nicely for what she made. She must be a hooker, they said. So she was dressed nicely, but she was white trash. They always contradicted themselves. But what would they say when they found out she'd gone to Kentucky? They'd start calling her a hillbilly hooker. How could they be so mean?

Well, it didn't matter. If they said anything, she'd sue this hospital, too. There was no reason she couldn't win two lawsuits.

Back at the convention center, Miranda saw that the remains of the storm were in Missouri now. New Orleans had long since been spared. When would they ever get home? She couldn't go forever without a paycheck.

She wondered if she should start flirting with one of the police officers guarding the evacuees. She could move up here and get married. Oh, why couldn't they get her a blow dryer? She'd never evacuate again without one.

Miranda put on one of her nice outfits and walked around and around the auditorium. Sure enough, one of the police officers, an Italian-looking man about 40, not too young, started following her. She smiled. She still had it.

She never flirted at work. The nurses did it all the time, but she'd been told flat out she'd be fired if she flirted. But she wasn't at work now.

The officer positioned himself so Miranda would have to walk right past him. Miranda smiled sweetly and blushed a little.

"Ma'am?"

Miranda frowned. She still preferred "Miss," but it had been a long time since she'd heard that title directed toward her. She still felt like a "Miss" inside, though.

"Good evening," she said in her Marilyn Monroe voice.

"You don't look like you belong here," he told her.

"My car is in the shop," she lied, "so I had to join the rest of the refugees."

"I figured it was something like that." He smiled. "Or you were working on a paper." He chuckled now. "I studied psychology before I joined the department."

"Oh, that was one of my best subjects," Miranda said. "My only bad subject was math."

"I was no good at math, either. That's why I ended up on the force instead of being a psychologist." He smiled again, and Miranda did, too. This was a guy who could really understand her. She felt a little thrill run through her body.

They walked along together and talked for half an hour. It was Miranda's first date in how many years? Watching Keith masturbate didn't count.

Miranda saw the other people sitting on their cots pointing at her, but she didn't care. This guy had a full head of hair, and he was tall, and he was good looking. He had everything she needed.

Finally, though, Miranda felt it was time to end the date. She'd read *The Rules*. She knew you were always supposed to leave the man wanting more. "I have to go to the bathroom now," she said. She obviously couldn't claim another commitment.

"Why don't you use the police officers' bathroom?" he suggested. "It'll be nicer."

Miranda smiled. He liked her. She followed him to the bathroom and went inside. Before she could get to the stall, however, she saw a huge sign posted over the sink. "Wash your hands after leaving the animal area. Stay healthy."

Miranda's mouth fell open. That was another lawsuit waiting to happen. She wished she had her cell phone with her so she could take a picture. Maybe she could get this guy to admit to other things like this. It wouldn't hurt to win two lawsuits. Or three, if she did go after that second hospital, too.

"How about tomorrow night I bring some take-out?" the officer asked when Miranda came out of the bathroom.

"That would be very nice," she said, smiling and lowering her eyes seductively.

She went back to her cot. The wheelchair lady glared at her, and the woman with TB coughed loudly in her direction. But Miranda smiled and pulled out a book to read. At least she'd been smart enough to bring some reading material along.

Miranda had a good night's sleep and had a fun time the next day at the Slugger bat museum with its huge bat towering over the building. When she walked next to two other women from the shelter, though, she heard one of them say to the other, "I hear she had sex in the bathroom."

Miranda couldn't believe it. Had the officer told everyone they'd had sex when she went in their bathroom? Men were such pigs. But she could take it. Keith had been a pig, too, and he'd even had the gall to marry someone else. Yet he'd kept seeing her up until two months before he died. Once she married this guy, she didn't care what he said. As long as he loved her. And she could tell he was well on his way toward that.

Miranda put on one of her other nice outfits when she got back to the convention center. Around 7:00, she saw the officer walking toward her. She smiled and moved over to meet him.

"In the mood for chicken?" he asked with a grin.

What was that supposed to mean? Did he think she was too old for him?

"In Kentucky?" she said, laughing. "I guess it's the law here."

She wasn't happy about getting her hands all greasy. Eating fried chicken always seemed so undignified. But the dinner went well, thank goodness. Last night, the officer had talked about himself. Tonight, he asked about Miranda, and though she wanted to maintain a mysterious aura, she found herself telling him everything, in exhaustive detail. She enjoyed having a captive audience, and besides, if he thought she was about to win a big lawsuit, he might be more inclined to marry her.

Miranda could see the concern on his face as she talked, and it touched her. No one had cared what she thought for a very long while. Maybe she really was going to find happiness after all this time. She felt her heart beating a little quickly, and it beat even faster when the officer took her hand.

"Miranda," he said gently, "it's been a long time since I was in class…"

She frowned. Did he want to go back to college on her settlement money?

"But it's clear you need some help. I'm not sure if you have borderline personality disorder or schizophrenia or are just delusional, but you need to see a doctor. Hasn't anyone ever told you this before? You're going to end up fired again, and no one is going to hire you, and you'll be living in places like this the rest of your life. You've got to get some help."

Miranda's mouth fell open. What did he mean by borderline personality? She had a wonderful personality. Was he crazy? How could he blame all that had happened on her? Hadn't he been listening? Was he just trying to be mean? Was he simply looking for a way to break up?

Then it dawned on her. He was a police officer, wasn't he? The police back home had contacted him, obviously. They were still after her even from a thousand miles away. She should have known all along something was up when he'd pretended to be nice to her.

"I do have a disease," she said sadly. "It's called head lice."

The officer withdrew his hand, and Miranda smiled.

"You say you've had this at least two years. Most people use a medicated shampoo and they're fine the next day. At worst, it takes two shampoos. You don't have head lice. Some people with mental illnesses are convinced they're infected with maggots internally. It's the same thing."

Miranda stood up, horrified. "You didn't just feed me maggots in that chicken, did you?"

The officer looked at her solemnly for a long moment. Then he stood up. "Good luck, Miranda," he said and walked off.

Good luck? What did he mean by that? Had he really put something in her food? What if she died up here in Kentucky? No one would ever find her. No one would ever know what had happened. Was the Church behind this? Was it the hospital?

Miranda hurried to the bathroom and forced herself to throw up. She tried to look in the toilet to see if there were any maggots in the mess, but she couldn't tell. But she should be okay, she thought. If she wasn't, she'd sue. The Louisville police would sure be sorry they'd messed with her.

Miranda walked back to her cot. As she passed the woman with TB, the woman coughed at her, and Miranda coughed right back.

"Hey!"

Miranda smiled and began deliberately scratching her head, even though it didn't itch.

No one bothered her.

She slept pretty soundly through most of the night, though she did wake up around 4:00 from her stomach growling. She felt the rumbles and wondered if that was just the gastric juices bubbling, or if it were maggots crawling. Damn that officer.

After breakfast, Miranda felt better. Everyone was carted off to the zoo today, and Miranda especially liked looking at the antelope and the parrots. She laughed as she realized just how right the Red Cross had been.

But when she got back to the convention center, the officials were rounding everyone up. They were finally going back to New Orleans. Thank god. Of course, by this time, there was probably another hurricane on its way. Or at least regular bad weather. Miranda was so tired of all the heat and mosquitoes and thunderstorms and termites and roaches in New Orleans. But maybe she'd meet a cute male flight attendant who had an apartment in another state. He'd see her on the plane and realize she didn't belong in this crowd and start talking to her and they'd start a romance in the air. She felt a thrill as she thought about it.

It was several more hours before Miranda's group boarded the bus. A cute man in his late thirties sat next to her, and he looked at her kindly and had nice smile lines on his face. Maybe she was going to have two romances on the flight. She was still desirable. That's why the other nurses didn't like her. "I'm a whale," the man offered with a grin. "How about you?"

"A shark," Miranda said, snapping her jaws playfully.

They began talking, and it turned out that the man's mother had been a nurse as he was growing up. "But she died several years ago."

"My parents are both dead, too," said Miranda, "but I get along okay."

"You look like a woman who knows how to get what she wants out of life."

Miranda smiled. She hadn't even mentioned the lawsuit yet, so he couldn't be after her for her money.

Miranda managed to sit next to him on the plane, making it look like a coincidence. She laughed, and the man did, too.

It was nighttime by now, and the man turned off his overhead light and nodded for Miranda to do the same. She felt a little thrill and switched off her lamp. A moment later, she felt a hand on her leg.

She was a good girl, so she wouldn't do anything even after they were dating. But she smiled now in the dim light. The evacuation had been a blessing, after all. God sometimes seemed to have it in for her, but he was coming through for her now.

She put her hand on top of the man's hand and squeezed. He in turn squeezed her thigh, and he leaned over to kiss her. Miranda allowed a quick peck and then pulled away, not wanting him to get the wrong idea, but she was happy.

Miranda was finally going to have a man, and a settlement, and she was going to have money and time to join a gym and lose some weight. Those nurses would sure be jealous. They would boil in their own juices knowing it was their meanness that had made it all possible. And she couldn't wait till she could walk back in the chapel and sit next to the Mormon doctor with a black man at her side. Maybe when he saw that other guys were interested in her, he'd leave his bitch of a wife. And maybe when the bishop saw that the Mormon doctor wanted her, the bishop would want her, too. Miranda giggled.

The plane headed down and down toward Miranda's new life. She sighed happily and drifted gently off to sleep, her hand still resting on her new boyfriend's hand. She dreamed of babies and balls and running horses, and she smiled a little in her sleep. She dreamed of all the clothes she could buy with her winnings, and how she'd parade around in front of all the other nurses. She dreamed of her new car and her new two-story house. She dreamed of the doctors who would court her, and the beautiful children her handsome husband would bring to the marriage. She murmured dreamily, nuzzling against the man sitting beside her. She slept on soundly till morning.

The Bishop's Confession

Bishop Randolph hated being a bishop. Yes, it was prestigious, and it was nice enough to have the respect, but the truth was, he wasn't worthy, and the guilt was too much to live with. Even since he'd studied in France for a semester abroad sixteen years earlier, he'd loved coffee. It wasn't the caffeine he was addicted to so much as the flavor. There were so many varieties, and he loved almost all of them.

With such Word of Wisdom problems, it had been hard to get a temple recommend so he could get married thirteen years ago. Keeping his recommend active all these years had been just as big a challenge. Bishop Randolph could go days or even weeks, sometimes a month or more, without coffee, but at some point, there would be an especially stressful day, and he would succumb. Coffee was simply too wonderful to pass up every single day of your entire life. It worried the bishop that this indicated he'd never be happy in the Celestial Kingdom even if he did manage to make it there. An eternity without coffee? Was he cut out for that?

Resisting had been hard enough even before he became bishop eight months ago, but now, with all the added stress, it had become a nightmare. It was all he thought about at work. And on the weeks he faltered, what was he supposed to do on Sunday? He couldn't very well abstain from partaking of the Sacrament. How would that look? So he just tried to see the stake president regularly and confess.

Lately, though, the stake president seemed to be demonstrating less patience with his weakness. "You're supposed to be an example, Ted. This commandment is designed for the 'weakest of all saints.' You've got to put this behind you."

So the bishop kept praying and fasting and trying just a little bit harder every day.

Today was Sunday, and he'd had an entire week without coffee. Of course, after a 7:00 a.m. planning meeting this morning before the three hours of services later, Bishop Randolph was feeling more and more that one little cup wouldn't be so bad.

Bishop Randolph was tired, but now that services were over, he had two hours of interviews to do. Every Sunday was simply pure hell. "Good afternoon, Brother Taylor," said the bishop, welcoming a man in his mid-forties into his office. "What can I do for you today?"

They chit chatted for a couple of minutes before Brother Taylor was able to relax and open up. "Some guys at work the other day told a really dirty joke, and I laughed at it. I didn't walk away or tell them it was inappropriate or anything. I just laughed."

"I see," said the bishop, nodding his head thoughtfully. "Well, what's done is done. But what do you think you could do differently the next time such a situation arises?"

A teenage girl, a Laurel, was next, and she wrung her hands over the fact that two days earlier, she'd received too much change back at the store and had kept it. Now she was afraid of getting the cashier in trouble if she brought the money back so late.

After this came a young returned missionary who couldn't keep from looking at women's breasts. He'd been caught staring twice this week. "Do you fantasize about women later and masturbate?" asked the bishop.

"Of course."

"Masturbation is a sin, you know, even if it *is* rather common among young adults."

"I'm just trying not to have sex. I'm not willing to give up whatever poor substitute I may have."

"Okay, but just try to sing a Church hymn when you get the urge, and see if that helps."

"All right, Bishop."

Another teenage girl came next, worried because her mother wasn't coming to church often enough, and then a 15-year-old boy being interviewed to be ordained as a priest next month, guiltily confessed he'd tried a cigarette a couple of weeks before.

"Believe me, nothing good comes from smoking," said the bishop. "It costs a ton of money, makes you too winded to climb stairs, and gives you cancer. There are other ways to be cool."

"I guess."

"So tell me, Jim, do you have any problems with masturbation?"

The leaders were really trying to crack down on self-abuse. It so often seemed a precursor to even worse sins. Talking about it was terribly dreary, though. Bishop Randolph felt that almost everyone seemed to indulge in this unseemly practice. Even he'd done it as a teen, but he'd learned to control himself on his mission, and he'd been good about it ever since. Even now, only having sex with Maureen once a week, he was able to control himself.

He smiled. He could control himself sexually, but the mere smell of coffee sent him over the edge. It was pretty pathetic. Still, he sincerely wanted to help the members of his ward lead better lives, and if he could help even just a few of the members make honest improvements, that would be something to be proud of.

Jim looked down at the floor.

"Yes, Jim?"

"Bishop, do—do we have to talk about this? It's embarrassing."

"All sin will be shouted from the rooftops on Judgment Day. It's better to stop sinning now and not be embarrassed in front of the entire world later."

Jim was still looking at the floor.

"How often, Jim?" asked the bishop gently.

"I dunno. Maybe three times a week."

"There! You see? Some boys do it every single day. There's real hope for you. I know this is uncomfortable to discuss, but what are your triggers? What makes you start fondling yourself?" At times, simply just talking about it with underage boys made Bishop Randolph feel like a child molester. But this was for the boy's own good.

Even with Jim's face looking downward, the bishop could still see him turning red. "I dunno," said the boy. "Sometimes, I just wake up in the night and...you know."

"Jim, that's even more good news. It means that while you're awake, you're in control of yourself. There are a great many boys who would be lucky to say that." He thought for a moment. "So if it's just in the middle of the night, I wonder…"

Bishop Randolph was quiet for another moment, and Jim shifted uncomfortably in his seat. "Jim, would it be possible for you to tie one hand to the bedpost before you go to sleep?"

Jim looked up at that, a little puzzled. "I guess so. Why?"

"Then you won't be as likely to touch yourself in your sleep."

"But—" Jim turned red a second time and looked at the floor again.

"What, Jim?"

"It's just that, well, I only *need* one free hand, if you know what I mean."

The bishop nodded. "I see your point." He paused. "Do you think you could ask your father to tie both your hands to the bedposts?"

Jim looked at the bishop in alarm. "Oh, I could never! He'd know why I was asking!"

"I see." The bishop rubbed his chin. It was so hard to come up with effective strategies for avoiding sin. Coffee was ubiquitous at work, but at least at home, the bishop could avoid temptation. The boy's penis, however, was with him at all times. "What about your older brother Clay?" he suggested. "I know he doesn't come to church much anymore. We'll have to work on that. But do you think he'd be willing to help you out?"

"I dunno. We used to be pretty close. But lately he just looks at me funny and won't speak to me."

"Will you ask him?"

"Okay. I suppose." Jim looked at his watch nervously. "Look, my Mom is waiting. If we take too long, she'll think…"

"All right. But let's talk again next Sunday and see how you're doing."

Just a couple more interviews, thought Bishop Randolph, and he'd be free for the day. He'd never realized how taxing it was to hear all the sins and worries and pettiness and hurts of so many people. Hearing each confession was like dying a little. Some days, he wanted to give up on the whole human race. And this was simply hearing from Mormons, who were perhaps the most righteous of all people. What must it be like for God, who heard all those prayers from millions of people of all religions, and saw everything even people who weren't praying were doing? Did he really want to become a god himself one day, the bishop wondered.

Soon Bishop Randolph was home, and he always made a point of playing Scrabble with the family after dinner on Sundays. Maureen had an English degree and worked as a substitute teacher. Kelly was twelve and a good student, so she liked to play. Scott was ten and would much rather play football, but the bishop forbade it on Sunday. They were good kids, but on Kelly's next birthday, she'd officially be a teenager, and Bishop Randolph wasn't much looking forward to the next few years.

On Monday, Bishop Randolph was back at work. He was a supervisor with Metro public transit. He'd always liked his job well enough. But since becoming bishop, he started seeing things in a new light. When a customer complained that a bus driver skipped her stop, or someone complained that a driver wouldn't make the bus "kneel" for him, when someone complained that the driver allowed some teenagers to play music too loudly, he felt he was back in the confessional. Complaints were confessions from the other end, but they were still confessions. He still saw the moral fragility of other people every day.

Today's biggest complaint was that one bus driver kept honking and yelling at other drivers all along his route. It wasn't the first time people had complained about Mario. The bishop would have to talk to him again.

As the day wore on, Bishop Randolph kept finding reasons to walk past the coffee pot. He resisted actually drinking, but it was a close call. The bishop wanted to give himself a treat every time he resisted, but the only treat he really wanted was a cup of coffee.

Family Home Evening that night went well. Maureen talked about how cleanliness was next to godliness, and after thanking the kids for their help in keeping the house clean, she mentioned that Sister Bradley was sick, and they'd have to clean her house for the next week or two. Scott rolled his eyes, but Bishop Randolph was pleased to see that this was the extent of the protest. Once the hormones started flowing in a couple of years, though, would his kids still be good? Hormones seemed to produce most of the world's misery. Sex, obviously, but even just plain old aggression and fighting were triggered by hormones.

If so much of the impulse to do evil was hormonal, Bishop Randolph wondered what percentage of responsibility the individual himself actually carried. Maybe a man was only 45% responsible for getting in a fight, only 23% responsible for fantasizing, only 11% responsible for making an irritable comment.

But hormones played no role in his desire for coffee. He was 100% on his own for that.

Work again was challenging on Tuesday. One of the drivers got in a minor accident but would still have to be drug-tested. Bill had tested positive for pot one time years ago, swore it was because of eating poppy seeds, and had passed all his screenings since. Was he cheating?

Wouldn't it be nice if there were some kind of test to show any of a hundred sins? Then the bishop wouldn't have to actually talk to his congregation, or at least, wouldn't have to listen to them.

At church that night, after a meeting with his counselors about Home Teaching statistics, he had two more interviews. "Bishop, I hit my wife," said a man about thirty, one of the outspoken men from the elders quorum.

"Why did you do that?"

"She always overcooks the broccoli. She knows I hate that."

"Is that worth hitting someone over?"

"It's the principle, Bishop. She isn't showing me respect."

"This is inappropriate behavior, Kevin. What can we do to help you control your impulses? Can you substitute hitting a pillow or taking a long walk?"

The next member was worse. Brother Tennant hemmed and hawed for almost fifteen minutes before the bishop could elicit the real reason for the visit. "I'm attracted to my daughter."

"Julia?" The bishop thought quickly. The girl was about thirteen.

Brother Tennant nodded. "I haven't done anything, of course. I wouldn't. But I think about it, and that makes me sick."

Bishop Randolph sighed. There was so much wickedness in the world. Brother Tennant had just been ordained a high priest not two months ago. And now this. "I'm going to recommend you see a counselor at LDS Social Services. If your insurance won't pay, we'll work something out."

"This is going on my record?" Brother Tennant looked aghast.

"A visit to a therapist will look a lot better on your record that a five-year-sentence at the penitentiary."

Brother Tennant nodded sadly, and they made the arrangements.

When he got home, the bishop went straight to bed. Maureen tried to engage him in conversation, but he just wasn't in the mood. Some 100% decaf coffee right now would be just perfect, he thought. He chewed on his pillow until he fell asleep.

Wednesday produced more trouble at work. Linda and Kim got into it. "You wear too much perfume," Linda complained. "You smell like a whore."

"I wouldn't know. I don't associate with whores. But you've got too much B.O. You shouldn't talk."

"I'm allergic to perfume. I've already reported it. If you keep wearing it, I'll bring disciplinary action."

"I *have* to wear perfume to keep from gagging every time you walk by smelling like a pig."

"I wouldn't know. I don't associate with pigs."

Bishop Randolph just stared longingly at the coffee pot.

Wednesday night after dinner, the bishop was back at church. The teenagers had an activity night, and the Single Adults were playing volleyball. Bishop Randolph saw Jim in the hallway and nodded, but the boy was with friends and pretended not to see him.

Karen, a young Single Adult woman about twenty-two, came to the bishop's office to talk. "My boyfriend's not a member," she said, "so he doesn't understand why I can't have sex." She hesitated. "He gets so impatient that I have to let him, you know, do it against me with his clothes on. That seems like a fair compromise, don't you think? A decent substitute?"

"Karen, you can't compromise at all with gospel principles. Something is either wrong or right."

"But he's such a good man. I'm sure I can convert him if we just go out a little longer."

"He'll never feel the Spirit while he's sinning, and you're helping him to sin."

"He's sinning less with me than if he was seeing someone else. *All* non-members are sinners, and hundreds of thousands of them still feel the Spirit enough to be baptized every year."

"You're rationalizing, Karen. You probably need to stop seeing this boy until after he gets baptized. If you tell him that, you'll see if he's serious about you or not. There's no substitute for true love."

Bishop Randolph wondered if the man's simply being baptized would change anything. The bishop was seeing every day that Church members were every bit as sinful as non-members. The idea saddened him, and he let out a deep sigh.

Maybe Jim, he thought. If he could just save Jim, he'd know he was a good bishop. He'd know he'd been forgiven about the coffee. He'd know he'd made a difference in the world.

Thursday at work, there were two major accidents in the city requiring the rerouting of two buses. There was road work in another location requiring yet another back-up route. And at a designated shift change, the relief driver for one line never showed up, and Bishop Randolph had one very tired, very angry bus driver on his hands.

That night was a miniature family night. The bishop had so little time with his family that he made sure to steal time for them whenever he could. Tonight they watched the Pixar movie *Up*. He liked kids' movies that were mature enough not to be insufferable for adults. He was sure that kept kids interested longer, too. Kelly and Scott seemed to enjoy the DVD, and Maureen did, too.

Bishop Randolph couldn't help but feel a little sad, though, when the childhood hero turned out to be a villain. But maybe it was good to prepare children for that inevitable fact of life.

The bishop looked over at the kids. How long could he keep them pure? Kelly almost had an adult body already.

He watched the closing credits showing the happy boy and happy old man, and when Maureen smiled at him, the bishop smiled weakly back.

Friday was another nightmare at work. A car had run over a bus sign and several people complained that the bus had passed them right up. Didn't the drivers know their own routes? What was taking the company so long to put the sign back up?

Another woman complained that a bus driver had deliberately splashed her, and then several people complained when a driver accidentally took the wrong exit and delayed everyone by twenty minutes before being able to turn around and get back to his original route.

At 1:35, Bishop Randolph had a cup of coffee.

It felt so good, so incredibly soothing going down that he had a second. Then he locked himself inside a bathroom cubicle and tried to force himself to pee it all out, but of course it wouldn't come. He'd almost made it a whole week, and now he'd have to talk to the stake president again. It would be humiliating to be released from his calling as bishop, but maybe that would be a blessing as well. He just had to help one of the other members before he left the position, though. Maybe Jim. The boy was still mostly innocent, still salvageable. He sure hoped he could help Jim.

Friday night, Bishop Randolph only spent an hour at church. He had to interview Brother Clarkson to talk him into paying tithing. He failed and couldn't help but suspect that the reason was simply that the Holy Ghost couldn't use him to bear witness, because of his sin earlier in the day. The bishop also had to interview a couple who were planning to be baptized the following day. They were about thirty, had one young child, and seemed nice enough. Bishop Randolph didn't press too hard, though. He didn't want to know their secrets.

He unfortunately did hear the secret the next man had. Brother Jeppson was a former elders quorum president with three children. "I look at porn almost every day. My wife is so fat, I can't help it."

"When was the first time you ever looked at pornography?" asked the bishop slowly.

"When I was twelve."

"And have you never looked at it again since then, till your wife got fat?"

"Well, no. Occasionally, I'd look. But now…"

"You shouldn't use your wife as an excuse, Brother Jeppson. Take responsibility for your own impulses. Don't use your wife as a substitute."

"I—I suppose you're right. But what am I to do?"

"Play sex games with your wife. Help her feel more attractive. She's probably embarrassed to be too sexual around you. Try to enjoy each other without judgment."

"I don't know, Bishop."

"There is lots of sexuality that *is* allowed to us. We just have to act within that framework."

"I'll try, Bishop."

"You know, in Polynesia, heavy women are often seen as sex objects. And you know that the painter Reubens was obsessed with heavy women. Most of his sexual paintings are about them. It's all in the way we look at things. If you think a thing is bad, then it is, regardless of the objective value of it. But whether or not being heavy is good, that's what you have to deal with, so it would be best if you could learn to like it. Others do, so you can, too." You can learn to *like* paying tithing, he wanted to say. You can learn to *enjoy* ten hours of General Conference in one weekend. You can learn to *love* home teaching. He forced a smile onto his face, feeling like the fraud he was.

Brother Jeppson left, looking unconvinced, and Bishop Randolph stared at his desk for ten minutes before getting up.

Back at home, the bishop had to deal with Scott, who'd gotten into a fight with another boy after school. Scott refused to say what it was over, and the bishop wasn't sure it mattered. He took away Scott's Nintendo and went to his bedroom to pray.

Saturday morning, Bishop Randolph slept in till 7:45. Then he had some toast with a glass of orange juice and headed over to the church. There was a work party today, involving the elders quorum, the high priests group, and the teenagers of the young men's program. They trimmed the hedges all over the church grounds and bagged all the clippings. Then they weeded the flowers. Most of the others left before the work was completed, but Bishop Randolph stayed. It felt incredibly good to deal with something clear cut. He felt wholesome again.

He went home to change and then came back for the 1:00 baptism. Presiding over that was so energizing, so hopeful. Maybe there really was a point to all of this.

There was just one interview after the baptismal service. Sister Ramsey knocked on the bishop's door nervously. "I think my daughter may be using drugs," she said worriedly. "Her grades have gone down, and she is so moody lately. I looked in her purse and found a red pill, and when I asked her what it was, she laughed and said it was a Tic Tac. But what do I know? I'm not going to eat it to find out."

"Just let her know you love her, and try to find some things she likes to do that you can do as a family."

"She hates us."

"I'm sure that's not true. You just need to find something she really likes and share that with her. Not buying clothes. Teenage girls like to do that with other teenage girls. But she must like Taco Bell, or shopping for posters, or going to the library..."

"Going to the library?"

"Or something. You know your daughter better than I do. You have to show her that being with family is more fun than being with other people. And the only way you can do that is to *make* being with family fun. She has to learn to see her family in a new light."

They talked a while longer, but the bishop was pretty sure that if the girl really were taking drugs, she was already a lost soul. Her ability to see her family anew was probably no longer an option.

Wasn't the gospel supposed to help people lead better lives? Sure, there was temptation to face in life, but why wasn't the gospel strong enough to stand up to it? Why was everyone so bad? Even now, all the bishop himself could think of was sneaking in another cup of coffee before he had to talk to the stake president the next day. Why was there so much human frailty? Could even the Atonement really make up for all of this? Even if they were all forgiven, weren't they still all miserable, weak creatures who would continue to sin despite their forgiveness, or at the very least still desire to sin, throughout eternity?

What good was it to be in heaven if you still wanted your cocaine? What good was it to be with the angels if you still wanted to look at pornography? What good was it to be creating your own worlds if all you really wanted was a cup of coffee? The Church taught that you had to overcome your weaknesses here in this life or they would follow you on to the next. That was why you couldn't do anything about them after you died, before the Resurrection, because you had no body to temper.

Your spirit would still have all those cravings, but without a body, you couldn't learn to suppress them.

But if you had a body now and still couldn't suppress them, what was going to be different after the Resurrection? You'd still have the same personality, the same spirit. Your body might be perfect, but you'd have the same weak, miserable soul you always had.

Bishop Randolph went home and tossed the football back and forth to Scott for half an hour. The boy wanted to play with his friends, though, so the bishop nodded and went back inside. He turned on some soothing music and sat in the living room with Maureen, but she was reading a book and turned the music off. He went in the bedroom and took a nap.

After dinner, Bishop Randolph watched a little TV with the family, and then he headed over to church to make an appearance at the youth dance. He saw Jim in the hallway. The boy looked nervous, but the bishop asked him if he still planned to stop by his office on Sunday afternoon. Jim nodded uncomfortably and hurried off.

Bishop Randolph sighed. If the boy were this nervous, he must still be masturbating. He was nevertheless a good kid, though, wasn't he? Did masturbating really change all that? Did having a cup of coffee really make you a terrible person? Was being a fat wife so awful? A little sin wasn't the end of the world. It just made you more human.

But Mormons weren't supposed to be human. "Be ye therefore perfect, even as your Father which is in heaven is perfect." Mormons were supposed to become gods.

Sometimes, the bishop wondered if people came to him for confession all the time just as a substitute for living.

Back at home, Bishop Randolph and Maureen made love. Then Maureen got up to make some hot chocolate and read some more. The bishop just lay in bed staring at the ceiling in the dim light streaming into the room from the street lamp outside.

Sunday morning began early as always with the planning meeting before services started. During Sacrament meeting, the bishop listened politely to the superficial talks about faith and prayer. After Priesthood meeting, he had one hour of interviews before he had to speak to the stake president himself. One young woman confessed she'd been to see an R-rated movie. Another admitted she'd eaten a rum-flavored pastry. And a newlywed man tearfully opened up about the fact that he was still masturbating, even though he now had a wife he could have legitimate sex with.

This just wasn't going to work. Bishop Randolph would have to use the coffee as an excuse, as a stand-in for his real reason, and ask the stake president to release him from his calling. Life was hard enough just seeing your own sins. It was unbearable to see everyone else's.

Finally, Jim knocked on his door and came in. It would have been nice to have had at least one victory before leaving office, Bishop Randolph thought sadly.

"How are you today, Jim?" asked the bishop with forced cheerfulness.

"I—I think I'm in love."

The bishop was startled. This threw things into a new light. Was he going to have to worry about heavy petting now, too? Or actual intercourse?

"Whoa. One step at a time. Let's talk about what we discussed last week first. Did you try having your hands tied at night? Did your brother help you?"

"Well…"

"Jim, I'm your friend. We can talk openly. Did you masturbate this week?"

"Not exactly." The boy squirmed in his seat.

"Did you *kind of* masturbate?"

Jim shrugged. "Last Sunday night, I asked Clay to tie my hands to the bedposts, like you said. But then…"

"Yes?"

"After he tied me up, he kept looking at me. He looked and looked, and then…"

"What happened?" The bishop's stomach was sinking.

"He tied my T-shirt around my mouth."

"Oh, my god."

"Then…then we had sex." He paused. "We've done it every night this week." The boy looked at the bishop imploringly. "It's okay, isn't it? We're brothers. We're already sealed to each other in the temple. It's okay if you're sealed, isn't it? I—I love him."

"You love him?" the bishop asked weakly.

"Yes, Bishop."

"Does he love you?" The bishop felt dizzy.

"Yes, Bishop." He looked up hopefully. "Does this mean he doesn't have to tie me up anymore?"

The bishop nodded in a daze. "Not unless you like it that way."

Jim giggled. The bishop stood up and put his hand on the boy's shoulder. "You can go now," he said softly. "But don't tell anyone else about this. Not the stake president. Not the next bishop. You understand?"

Jim frowned. "Okay."

They shook hands and the boy left the office. Bishop Randolph sat back down and stared at the desk. It was time to go see the stake president. The bishop considered just skipping out and heading straight for Starbucks, but he decided that would be rude. He walked down the hall and knocked on the president's door.

"Hi, Ted. How are you today?"

"I don't think I'm cut out to be a bishop, Ken."

"Nonsense."

"I want to be released."

The stake president was silent for a long moment. "Well, Ted, the truth is we don't have anyone else we could call right now. Do you think you could hang on for another year?"

"Another year?" The bishop's head felt foggy.

"Yes. Just a little while longer. The Lord needs you."

Bishop Randolph stared at the floor for a couple of minutes.

"Ted?"

"Sure, Ken, I can hang on."

"That's the spirit."

They shook hands, and the bishop walked slowly out to his car. He drove off the church grounds and headed right past Starbucks without stopping. He pulled into a Safeway parking lot and walked calmly into the store. After a moment, the bishop found the right aisle and picked up a can of Folgers. He could smell the coffee beans everywhere on this aisle. He breathed deeply and smiled, and finally he headed for the cash register.

The next stop was Walgreens to buy a coffee pot, and then the bishop turned his car toward home.

A Life of Their Own

"**D**r. Taylor, my breasts feel funny." Sister Anderson was one of my patients who was also a member of my ward. Even as a busy plastic surgeon, I had been called two years ago to be our ward's lay bishop. I'd devoted my life to fixing wrongs in the form of car accident scars and mastectomies, but the last two years I'd had to balance that with worrying about the spiritual wrongs my congregants were facing. It created a kind of coexistence in my soul of acting as both a physical and a spiritual healer. Jesus had done both, too, I reflected, so I was well on my way to becoming like him. My brother Theo certainly liked to crucify me whenever he had the chance.

"What do you mean, Valerie?" Sister Anderson liked to be called by her first name in my office. This always felt a little awkward for me, as she was the stake president's wife, and the stake president was a notch higher than I was, head over eight congregations while I presided over only one. I'd put breast implants in Sister Anderson over a year ago due to stage two cancer. It was always exciting to turn a death sentence into a reason for living.

"I don't know. They—they tingle. You don't think they've burst? You don't suppose the cancer is back?" I'd seen hickeys on the necks of many teenagers over the years, but Sister Anderson was the only person I knew with hickeys on her breasts. I expected they tingled a lot.

"You're only one month away from your scheduled check up. Let's go ahead and do some tests today."

We did the tests, but I was pretty sure the symptoms were all in Sister Anderson's mind. She was one of those Mormons who'd bought a generator in case all the world's computers stopped working in 2000. She had a year's supply of food stored underneath her stairwell. Her husband made $70,000 annually, and yet she still sewed most of her own clothes. When doing her genealogy, she came across an ancestor's name in the family tree frontispiece of a novel she was reading and incorporated the history of the fictional family into her own family group sheets.

She was also one of those Mormons who was already half living in the afterlife. When I'd reconstructed her breasts, she told me she was worried about how this would affect her ability to bear spirit children later when she became a god and needed to nurse them. I assured her as her bishop that she'd be resurrected with her original breasts intact. She asked if she could be resurrected with larger ones, for her husband's sake. I thought it might be better if he was simply resurrected with smaller hands, or a smaller mouth.

It would be unlikely, I thought, that Sister Anderson's gel implants had burst or begun leaking and causing some kind of connective tissue disorder. That had been only a minor problem even in the old days, before a moratorium on using them was imposed back in 1992. For the next fifteen years, women could only get this type of implant if they were part of a study, but since 2006, they were common practice again. The difference was that the bag they were in now was thicker and stronger. It made the implants feel a little less natural, but they were also pretty darn secure, no matter how rough President Anderson might be with them.

"When will the results be back, Bishop? I mean, Doctor?"

"You know how this works, Valerie. It'll be a couple of days. I'll give you a call."

"But the X-ray looks normal?"

I hesitated. Actually, the X-ray didn't look normal at all. In fact, it didn't look like anything I'd ever seen before. Not ruptured. Not cancerous. But not normal. I didn't want to say anything, though, until the other results were back. No sense worrying the poor woman for nothing.

"Let's reschedule you for a week from today, just in case we need to do something more. In all likelihood, I'll be giving you a call in a few days with an all clear, and we'll cancel the appointment, but it won't hurt to have some time set aside as a back up." Naturally, if there were any sign of cancer, I'd send her back to her oncologist, but she'd come to me this time, and I could at least run these preliminary tests.

"You *do* think something's wrong."

"Let me just feel them one more time."

Sister Anderson always looked uncomfortable when I put my hands on her breasts. She seemed to feel she was committing adultery. I wanted to reassure her that a doctor's physical exam was not a sexual act, but she seemed to need to feel extra righteous in a way that assumed all physical contact was forbidden, so I just lifted and pressed and felt in silence.

"Oh."

"What, Bishop? I mean, Doctor."

"Nothing."

"What?"

I laughed. "It's just that you moved. It made it feel like your breasts twitched."

"I didn't move."

I shrugged. I wasn't going to make a federal case of it.

Sister Anderson leaned forward and whispered. "They seem—they seem to have a life of their own." She looked around as if someone might be listening. "Some days, they're perky and some days they droop. And it has nothing at all to do with...with...you know."

I nodded. "I'm sure everything is fine. But I'll call you as soon as I know, one way or the other."

"All right."

"Any plans for the rest of the day?"

"I'm going to help my granddaughter sell Girl Scout cookies, and then I'll study for Gospel Doctrine. I always like to know the answers for class on Sunday."

After she left, I stared at the X-ray for a long while.

I thought about why Sister Anderson had wanted breast implants in the first place. She was in her early 50's, married thirty years, and didn't need to look sexy any more. But as prudish as Mormons could be, we also had an odd streak of sexual obsession. We believed if we were righteous enough in this life, we'd be rewarded a place in the Celestial Kingdom with our partner and enjoy a sexual relationship for eternity. Only the super righteous would reap this particular reward. All others would have celibacy enforced upon them throughout the eons.

But the gift of everlasting sex came with a price tag. We would have to create our own worlds and run those planets as our God ran ours. Obviously, we'd have to people the planets by having millions, even billions, of spiritual offspring who then went to the planets to gain physical bodies. And we'd also have to create the mountains and oceans and birds and maybe experiment first by creating our own dinosaurs and other creatures as well. My wife Sally and I even discussed some of the animals we might like to create some day. People would always be people, of course, but we could play around a little with the animals. Sally was adamant about creating colored fur. She absolutely thought green fur would function as camouflage, but she insisted we try purple and red at least once to see how it would work. "Birds and fish have all these brilliant colors. Why can't we try it with mammals, too?" She liked to talk about all kinds of different possibilities that we could develop while populating our planets. Flying cats. Dogs with arms as well as legs. Flowers that could transplant themselves if they needed to find better soil conditions.

I, however, was mostly hoping that somehow once we were on the other side of the veil, sex would become a little more interesting again, as it had been when we first got married. If it was sometimes stale now after only twenty years, what would it be like after a thousand? Ten thousand? A million? At times, Sally and I pretended I was raping her, or that she was the prophet's wife, or a patient under anesthesia, or whatever else we could think of. It occasionally disturbed me that I could get an erection even when Sally was pretending to be a corpse. Did gods play sex games to liven up the Celestial bedroom, too? Even with the possibility of eternal polygamy, I wanted some promise of excitement, or the blessing of sex might end up a curse. Was that why God so often seemed in a bad mood?

Still, if the alternative was everlasting celibacy, I was determined to be worthy of the Celestial Kingdom and not just the Terrestrial or, God forbid, the Telestial.

I called Sister Anderson on Friday. "There's no sign of cancer," I said simply, "and no suggestion of leakage, though we really can't be sure of that without doing something a little more invasive."

"Perhaps we'd better then."

"What's wrong?"

"Bishop Taylor, I mean, Doctor Taylor, I've—I've had—" She paused a long while. "My nipples have this crusty stuff on them now all the time. It was just a little bit before. I thought it was dirt at first, that I wasn't bathing well enough. But it's worse now. Oh, this is so embarrassing."

That sounded like an infection more than anything else, but Sister Anderson's white count had been normal.

"You were scheduled for Tuesday, but do you think you could come back in today?"

"Oh, thank you, Doctor."

Sister Anderson was at my office by noon, and I skipped lunch to squeeze her in. I took scrapings of the odd, gritty substance that seemed to be oozing from her nipples, and I prescribed an antibiotic. I palpated her breasts again, longer this time, once more feeling an odd twitch, and I scheduled an MRI for the following week.

"I'm sure it's just an infection," I said, "but the MRI will tell us more. I'll analyze this grit and call you when I know something. Your MRI is on Tuesday, so I'll cancel your appointment with me that day and have you come in Wednesday."

"I'll be okay by Wednesday, won't I?" said Sister Anderson a little nervously. "Wednesdays and Saturdays are the days Geoff and I—the days we—well, my husband likes to suck on them and…"

"You may have to do the sucking this next week."

"Oh, Bishop Taylor!"

I sent the scrapings to the lab right away, and before I left for the day, I had my answer. They were tiny nodules of silicon dioxide.

I was stumped. There was silicon in the grit, but silicon gel implants certainly weren't made of silicon dioxide, so I couldn't see how this might be related to a leak. Was Sister Anderson just playing with me, putting sand on her nipples and coming in so that I would put my hands on her? Maybe this was her way of having an innocently illicit affair.

But her breasts had in fact felt funny, I remembered, and that X-ray was definitely odd. The MRI would tell me more, but I called up my brother Theo now.

"Victor? What's up?"

"Theo, I have a chemistry question for you." My brother was a chemistry professor at the university, the "smart" one in the family, though I earned four times as much even in a bad year.

"Sure. What do you have for me?"

"Well, you know silicone gel implants are just made out of silicone, right?"

"It's silicon mixed with oxygen, hydrogen, and carbon, yes. It's a middle molecular weight substance as a gel. If it were a low molecular weight, it would be an oil rather than a gel, and at a high molecular weight, it would be a rubber. You can do all kinds of things with silicon."

"Yeah, well." I remembered now why I only talked to him every couple of months, though we lived in the same town. He was always trying to show how superior he was to me. Well, I was the bishop, wasn't I? He was only elders quorum president in his ward. I had a son serving a mission in Kenya now. Theo's son smoked pot and hardly ever went to church. Theo was never going to end up a god.

"So what's your question?"

"Could the silicon leaking turn into silicon dioxide?" I asked.

"What an odd question."

"Well, I have this patient who seems to be oozing silicon dioxide from her nipples."

There was silence on the other end of the line.

"Theo?"

"I wonder…"

"What?"

"Victor, I'm just about finished here for the day. Can you stay at your office a little longer? I'd like to take a look at your test results. I assume you've taken an X-ray?"

"Of course."

"Is it okay if I stop by in about half an hour?"

"You really think you know what's going on?" It would be irritating if he was the one to figure out the answer, but it was why I'd called, wasn't it? A true Latter-day Saint looked for truth wherever it could be found, even if I had to swallow my pride in front of my know-it-all brother.

"Maybe."

"I have to get home for dinner early so I can get over to the church tonight. You know how it is being bishop."

"Sure. Sure. I'll be over in a few minutes."

I studied the test results again and looked at the X-ray another time, trying to come up with an answer before Theo showed up. I was still stymied when he arrived, and I explained the case as best I could.

"What do you make of this?" Theo pointed to an area of light streaks on the X-ray.

"It doesn't look normal," I admitted, "but I've seen lots of pictures in textbooks of leakage, and it doesn't look like that, either."

"Does it look intact?"

I paused. "No," I admitted. "I suppose I'd better go in and see if there is leakage. I just don't know."

"Could this be silicon fibrils?" asked Theo, pointing.

"Fibrils? I don't see how. Gel doesn't turn into fibrils, even if it does leak."

"It could if her breasts have come alive."

I stared at Theo. Was he serious? Probably he was trying to pull my leg so he could make fun of me later. It wouldn't be the first time. "Do you use the same drug dealer your son goes to?" I bit my lip, but Theo didn't seem to react.

"All life on Earth is carbon-based," said Theo, "because carbon is tetravalent. It can form four bonds because of its outer electron shell. It usually bonds with other carbons, or oxygen, hydrogen, or nitrogen."

"I know what tetravalent means. I went to medical school, you know."

"So you realize that silicon is also tetravalent. It's right under carbon in the periodic table."

"What has that got to do with my patient's breasts?"

"We've tried thousands of ways to try to create silicon-based life, always without success. But sooner or later, it's possible it will just develop spontaneously on its own, just like carbon-based life had to do at some point."

"And you think the first sign of life will be in a middle-aged woman's tits?"

"Oh, I seriously doubt it. But I always keep my eyes open. I wouldn't mind winning a Nobel prize."

"What about me? She's *my* patient, after all."

"Okay. Okay. I just want you to do some tests that won't hurt her breasts if, well, if they *are* alive."

Theo explained what he wanted me to do, and I called Sister Anderson to ask her to come in Monday before her Tuesday MRI. She seemed anxious to comply, and on Sunday, she pulled me aside after Sacrament meeting. "Can we meet in the Bishop's office?"

"I have to interview one of the deacons." His mother was concerned about him masturbating, wasting his seed needlessly. Frankly, unless the mother intended to send her son to a fertility clinic every week for the next ten years, the boy wasn't going to be using his seed for anything else much more useful.

"Can you reschedule?"

"Sure."

I took the boy into my office and closed the door. "Your sperm may well have a life force in addition to its fertile properties," I said bluntly. "And bringing it forth a couple of times a week will only make you feel more alive than not doing it, so I wouldn't worry about it." It was one of the inconsistencies I found in Mormon attitudes toward sexuality. Only sex within marriage was acceptable. I could accept that extramarital sex was wrong, but what of amarital sex? If you were unmarried, you weren't allowed to be sexual even with yourself. I did hope I was up to the challenge of Celestial sexuality, but I very much wanted to believe I wouldn't be left completely out in the cold if I didn't make it. And if we only had these few years on Earth to be sexual, I didn't want to deprive this boy of what little time he had. If he wasn't even dating yet, I figured it was safe enough to let him beat off once in a while. Perhaps it was a sin to have non-procreative sex, but lots of older married couples did it all the time, so what was so bad about a young person doing something non-procreative?

At best, we only created six or seven other lives while we were here on Earth. Sally and I had just three children. We had been looked down on for years for our lack of commitment in bringing forth life. Theo had four children, but after my three, I just didn't want any more. I was afraid this left me a less than Celestial person, so I'd sneaked off to a fertility clinic myself a few times to donate. I always bought Sally a little gift with the money I made. It was right after my twelfth visit that I was called to be a bishop. I couldn't help but feel there was a connection.

I smiled at the boy, and he turned red as I leaned over toward him. "Just don't let your Mom catch you anymore." He nodded, and I shooed him out of the office quickly and then ushered Sister Anderson in.

"Bishop, I'm concerned."

"Do you have any new symptoms?"

"Look."

She unbuttoned the front of her dress and let it fall off her shoulders. Then she pulled off her top garment. When I saw Mormon underwear in my physician's office, I didn't think much about it. But seeing them now in my bishop's office, I couldn't help but focus on the little symbols over the nipples, the L to symbolize an arm raised to the square, to remind us to remain righteous always, and the V to remind us of a compass, so that we'd keep ourselves focused on our ultimate goal and destination.

"I don't see anything."

Sister Anderson sighed in frustration. "Bishop, they're *bigger.* They're swollen."

"Do they hurt?"

Sister Anderson shook her head. "They feel fine. In fact, they feel better than ever. There's always a warm, tingly sensation that makes me feel—they feel fine."

I palpated her breasts. They didn't feel quite normal, but I couldn't put my finger on exactly what was different. It reminded me of my first attempts at phlebotomy. I'd palpate someone's arm to feel their veins, and even when I could physically see the vein I was touching, I couldn't feel anything with my fingers at first. It took a great deal of practice before I could detect veins with my fingertips. I had the feeling that if I just knew what I was looking for, I could feel it in Sister Anderson's breasts now.

"Sister Anderson, I have a delicate question." I couldn't call her Valerie in church.

"Yes?"

"Have you and President Anderson ever done anything...strange...to your breasts since the implants?"

Sister Anderson blushed. "Well, naturally Geoff put his hands on them and gave me a blessing with his consecrated oil, that they'd be as lifelike as if they were real."

"Uh huh."

"And, you see, Geoff has this machine with electrodes he puts on his muscles to make them contract. It's his way of exercising while we watch TV. Only PBS, of course."

"Of course."

"So anyway, we put the electrodes on my breasts a couple of times to see if, well, you know."

I really didn't, but I nodded.

"And Geoff's sister is an herbalist, so one day she gave me vitamin injections."

"In your breasts?"

She nodded. "We really wanted my breasts to be as normal as possible. Geoff loves them so."

I shook my head. "But a needle may have punctured them, Sister Anderson. They might very well be leaking."

"Oh, dear."

There was a knock on the door, and I felt a rush of adrenalin. What if I were discovered in my office with a half-naked woman? I'd be released as bishop. I might even be excommunicated. Wouldn't Theo love that?

"Who is it?" I asked through the closed door.

"It's President Anderson. Is Valerie in there?"

I opened the door a crack, and since no one else was in the hall, I quickly let him in and locked the door again. President Anderson walked over to his wife and gave her a peck on the lips. She was still unclothed, and I felt awkward, but I put my hands back on her left breast.

"Let me try one more time to feel what might be going on."

As I palpated Sister Anderson's left breast, President Anderson felt her right one, smiling. I started sensing an erection and hoped it wouldn't show through my suit pants.

"What do you think?"

I shook my head. "Maybe it's a little spongier than gel-like. We'll do more tests tomorrow. If you're feeling well, there's certainly no emergency, whatever may be happening. Everything's going to be okay."

Sister Anderson put her clothes back on, the three of us said a prayer together for the health of her breasts, and then the two of them left. I sighed and let in my next congregant, a computer geek who kept getting in trouble for creating viruses.

Sister Anderson was due in my clinic office at 10:00 the next day, and since my 9:00 canceled when I got in at 8:30, I called Theo to see if he wanted to come by earlier so we could talk. I told him what I'd learned yesterday, letting slip who the patient was, and he laughed.

"You think it's funny that she may be leaking?"

"Victor, she's a wonderful experiment."

"She's a person."

"Okay. Okay. But just think about it. Silicon makes up over 25% of the Earth's crust. It's everywhere. And it's not like it isn't already utilized by other life forms. Diatoms use it as a component in their cell walls. Lots of plants, especially grasses, use it in metabolism."

"So you're back to believing her breasts are alive?"

Theo shrugged, still smiling. "Did she have sand on her nipples at church yesterday?"

"Yes."

"The biggest reason silicon doesn't seem to be used in most life forms is because of the difficulty it has in oxidizing. When carbon oxidizes during respiration, it forms carbon dioxide as waste, which is fairly easy to get rid of. But silicon forms silicon dioxide—sand—and a solid is a lot harder to eliminate."

I was confused. "So you think…"

"All that sand coming from her nipples, who knows? I still don't see how even if those implants had come to life, how they'd be able to use someone's body structures for their own benefit. Symbiosis is usually an evolved process, not a first-time event. But perhaps this thing is parasitic rather than independent."

I still wondered if Theo was pulling my leg. "Wouldn't something like that be too alien to coexist with us?"

He shook his head. "I don't see why. It's harmless enough. That's why you use silicon in the first place. We already use it in the body in lots of other ways. It's used in artificial joints and heart valves, as a tissue expander, as prostheses for the skeletal system, in ophthalmology, in penile prostheses, like the one you need."

"But life?"

Theo shrugged. "Silicon is used as a facilitator in nerve regeneration. I guess it could happen."

I frowned. "Doesn't life grow? Won't it reproduce? Are we going to have baby breast implants running around?"

"We'll have to deal with that when we get to it. Maybe it would have a maximum adult size. Or perhaps we'd need to do a Caesarian on her breasts."

"Maybe we should just try to take the whole thing out right now. I could schedule her for surgery."

"It might not be able to live on its own."

"How do we test for life when all our tests are based on assuming a carbon base?"

"The real question is what we're going to name this new species. I was thinking *Theophilus silicansis.* What do you think?"

"*You* get to name it?"

"You want it to be called *Victorianus something-or-other?*"

"It doesn't have to be *–anus.*"

"Okay. Okay. How about *Senogenitus silicansis*?"

"Hmm." I thought for a moment. "Maybe."

Theo laughed. "You know, Patricia and I have talked about creating silicon-based life on our own planet one day."

Like he'd ever make it to the Celestial Kingdom with that shrew of a wife, I thought. I tried not to snort. "Well, *I'm* the one who put those implants in."

"Yes, but it was President and Sister Anderson who brought them to life, and me who discovered it."

"Whatever."

We talked for another fifteen minutes until Sister Anderson arrived. Theo refused to leave the examination room. "Oh, hi, Brother Taylor," Sister Anderson said nervously.

"Do you mind if my brother takes part in the exam?" I asked. "He's a chemist and may be able to offer some insight into what may be going on chemically."

"I suppose that would be all right."

"I'm going to need a biopsy, and in addition to your MRI tomorrow, I've also scheduled you for a CT scan afterward."

"Do you think the cancer is back?"

"No, we think..." I paused. "...some unique biological process may be occurring."

Sister Anderson frowned. "Well, my breasts feel even larger today than they did yesterday. Geoff seems to like that well enough, but all this grit is driving him to distraction."

"Perhaps you should wear a bathing suit and pretend you're on a beach, like in *From Here to Eternity*. Some men find sand sexy."

"My brother has a poor sense of humor," I said. "Sister Anderson, let's get on with the exam. Would you mind disrobing?"

"In front of your brother?"

I nodded and she complied reluctantly. Theo's face was as eager and excited as a schoolboy's. There was a reason the Church didn't approve of members drinking Coke, but Theo felt he was above such rules. Pride was always one of his weaknesses. He could learn a thing or two about humility from me, but he was always so sure he was best. When it was clear that Theo and I were heading for different career paths, my mother had said, "It's good for the boys to have lives of their own." But I could tell she secretly favored Theo.

As I prepared the biopsy needle, Theo approached Sister Anderson. She eyed him warily.

"I've just got to feel for myself," he said. It wasn't a request for permission. He reached over and gently squeezed Sister Anderson's right breast.

"Bishop Taylor—"

"It twitched! I felt it twitch!"

"Theo, get a hold of yourself."

"*Senogenitus silicansis*. I'll be famous."

"*We'll* be famous."

"Bishop Taylor?"

"*I* discovered this. You don't know enough freshman chemistry to make any connections. *I* get the credit because I deserve it."

"Like hell." I pulled Theo away from Sister Anderson.

"I'll bet there's even chirality. Look, her right breast is probably the mirror image of the left. What a breakthrough that would be if it was happening at the molecular level."

"I want you to leave now, Theo."

"I won't. I'm taking part in every test from now on. *I'll* make the determination. You were always the leech. You'd never have made it through med school without me. I wrote half your papers."

"Theo, you promised never—"

"Bishop Taylor?"

I walked to a drawer and opened it, pulling out a scalpel. I showed it to Theo. He laughed. "You need to leave," I said. "This is my patient, my implant, my discovery. I'm taking the credit. We'll see who becomes famous."

"What are you two fighting about?"

"Your breasts are alive. It's a new species. A new order of life altogether. Nothing like it has ever existed on this planet before."

"Shut up, Theo. I'll handle this."

"I knew it! I felt something the instant Geoff gave me a blessing."

"Well, *he's* not taking credit!" I said quickly. "Hey!" I hadn't noticed, but Theo had moved toward a drawer, and now he had a scalpel, too.

"Take the biopsy," said Theo. "Let's get these tests done. One for your lab, and one for mine."

"I thought I was going to be an android or something, but this is even better."

"Get out, Theo."

"I'll do the biopsy myself."

"Bishop Taylor, I don't want any more tests."

I lunged at Theo and slashed down at his arm, drawing blood in a long line. I felt a tingling in my groin. Theo shouted and lunged back, cutting a slice across my chest. He cut my nipple. For some reason, this seemed more insulting than just cutting regular skin. I was so mad I thrust again, stabbing Theo in the stomach. Blood spurted from the wound. Theo waved his scalpel and ripped half my ear off.

Sister Anderson stood off to the side squealing while I tried everything I could to kill Theo. He was Jacob, plotting to steal my birthright. Sister Anderson would testify for me in a Church court, and I wouldn't be excommunicated. She'd testify for me in a secular court, too. *I* was her doctor. *I'd* saved her breasts. *I'd* saved her marriage because of the implants. That bastard Theo was trying to ruin everything, just like he'd done when he told my first fiancée' I wasn't a virgin and then dated her himself. Here I'd actually created life and he just wanted to confiscate it for himself. I never did trust PhD's.

And Mom and Dad had bought *him* a house when he graduated, when all they got me was a car.

I lunged again and sank the scalpel into Theo's neck. He kicked me and stabbed into my chest. He slipped on some blood and fell to the floor, but he didn't get up. I leaned over him, panting heavily. "I—brought—forth—life," I wheezed. Then I fell next to Theo on the floor. My hand was resting on his chest, and he picked it up with disgust and thrust it away.

I lay on the floor, my blood mixing with Theo's. I hoped Sister Anderson would go alert my secretary and get me help. I looked up at her. She was staring down at her breasts, petting them softly. "Sister Anderson," I managed to say but could get no further.

"Come on, my babies," she said, pulling her clothes up over her breasts, "let's go home and talk to Daddy."

I watched weakly as Sister Anderson picked up her purse. She walked over and stood above me. "You know, Bishop," she said slowly, "it's not really like having a baby. That's more like…like a prolongation of your own life. This is creating entirely new life. I bet Geoff and I get translated soon. We won't even have to wait for the resurrection. We're practically gods now."

She started to turn away and then looked back. "I'll have Geoff come to the hospital and give you guys a blessing. Maybe some part of you will come to life, too."

"Maybe his brain," whispered Theo.

"Maybe his heart," I panted back.

"Maybe his balls," Theo grunted.

I realized then that my penis had been hard throughout the entire fight. It was starting to wilt now, and I worried again about my chances of enjoying eternal erections. Surely, the act of creating life would outweigh my attempt to eradicate it, especially since I was so completely justified. Life simply had to trump death. That must be why I could get a hard-on even while attacking my brother. The life force had to show its superiority.

I was feeling very sleepy. I looked over at Theo, who was already asleep. Sister Anderson was walking out of the office, and I looked up at the light in the ceiling, thinking of God.

Perhaps after I recovered, I could go to another plastic surgeon and get a silicon prosthetic enlargement for my penis, and maybe I could get it to come to life, too. And even though Sally's breasts were perfectly healthy, I could put some implants in her as well.

I was going to be a god. I was going to be famous. *Victorianus* my ass. *Senogenitus* might be okay for the breasts, but I'd call my living penis *Victoropenosis silicansis* or something similar.

This was just the beginning. Because of this, I might even be promoted in the Church to apostle, and who knows, maybe even prophet one day. I was a great man, as I always knew I would be. Who was Theo to judge? He didn't even pay a full tithe. And he had bad breath, too.

I heard a scream and looked up to see my secretary, Ann, staring down at me in horror. But I felt okay. Just a little tired. Being a god was hard work. I smiled up at Ann. Then I closed my eyes, and, dreaming of the awards I was bound to win, I gently fell asleep.

Noseless Lesbian Murderers

"Okay, class," said Lois, raising her hand to shush the students, "today we're writing another in-class essay." There was a groan, though she'd announced this on Monday. "The argument today is 'Is it healthy to shield children from worldliness?'" There was another long groan. "Whichever side you pick, remember to have at least three pros and one significant con that you deal with. Don't just see your own side of the argument. That isn't logical, and we need to be logical to deal effectively with life." She paused a moment and then smiled wearily. "Okay, everyone, you can begin."

Lois sat down and started grading the essays from her earlier class. She taught one general composition and three advanced composition courses here at BYU-Idaho. Lois preferred the advanced comp courses because they dealt with argument. So often, the students would complain that composition courses weren't relevant to their lives, that they'd never need to write a single composition in their entire careers. But at least with argument, Lois could insist that logical thinking was simply a strong life skill that would benefit them no matter what lay in their future.

The problem was, of course, that no matter how hard she tried, the kids never seemed to grasp the concept of logic. It irritated her. What was it about Mormons that made them so resistant to such innately human thought? This was, after all, what separated man from the beasts in the first place. It wasn't their soul. Even animals had souls.

Lois graded quickly. It took her about eight minutes to read, critique, and evaluate a paper. She was able to get through seven of her stack of twenty-six essays before the class was over. Of course, now she had an additional batch of twenty-seven more. It would be a long day. She hoped she could get most of the work done before Gerald came home.

Lois had no office at the university because she wasn't a regular staff member. She and Gerald were service missionaries. They'd sent their papers off to Salt Lake eight months ago, expecting to proselytize in Rome or Athens. Even when the bishop suggested they teach English instead, Lois had envisioned Kenya or Guatemala. To be called to teach college English to Mormon students in Idaho had been a real blow, but Gerald had simply said, "When ye are in the service of your fellow beings, ye are only in the service of your God."

Lois had earned a Masters in English umpteen years ago, feeling daring to study things as worldly as Chaucer and Swift, but she'd been a stay-at-home Mom for over twenty years. And Gerald had been a successful businessman back in Omaha. *His* call to service was to be a janitor here for two of the local church meetinghouses. He'd accepted the call humbly, but Lois had petitioned to change the assignment. Now Gerald worked in the temple as custodian as well. Gerald stayed very busy, unfortunately, but that was what service was all about, wasn't it? Lois had hoped for something a little more sophisticated, perhaps working with homeless people, or battered women, or even, she thought wistfully, unwed mothers.

"See you Friday, Sister Brady."

The comment drew Lois back to her departing class. "Oh, have a nice day, Shawn."

"Sister Brady, I know this is a Church school, but do all our topics have to be Church-related, just because you're a missionary? There's a whole world out there beyond the Church, you know."

"I *do* know," she said. "What I'm trying to teach, though, is logic. You won't be able to face the world without logic to keep you in the Church." Lois smiled, but she felt like an imposter saying such things, like a child playacting at being a grown-up.

Shawn grimaced but nodded and left. Lois then gathered up her things and went in search of an empty classroom. She liked to do as much of her grading away from the apartment as possible. It allowed the tiny one-bedroom she and Gerald rented to be at least some sort of haven from the world.

Funny that she needed a haven when she lived in a Mormon town.

She thought of their three-bedroom home back in Omaha that she and Gerald were renting to strangers for the eighteen months they'd be in Idaho. She hoped her carpets wouldn't be ruined. But even if they were, it was all for the glory of God.

She stopped. What if the renters were drinking alcohol in their house? What if the husband was having an adulterous affair? What if the wife was?

Lois almost felt a little envious of the freedom those living in ignorance had.

She finished one batch of essays and plowed halfway through the second before she stopped and piled the rest in her bag. If she looked at one more inane paper, she'd go crazy. Maybe the Church was right about her call, if this service saved some other poor soul from having to teach. Being a teacher wouldn't be so bad if there wasn't so much grading involved, but how else could the students really learn except to write? And how could they improve without critiques? Really, the class needed to meet every single day, and she should assign one essay per week. But saint or no saint, Lois wasn't up to grading hundreds of sophomoric essays from four classes.

Well, really, they were freshmanoric, weren't they? These were freshman level classes, after all. So perhaps she was expecting too much. The boys were hardly even shaving yet.

Still, the job was a challenge. She wasn't just trying to get by in life. She wasn't after a paycheck. She was called by God to make the world a better place.

She sighed and pulled the rest of the ungraded papers out of her bag and started reading again. She'd critique these essays so well the students couldn't help but learn. They'd be better missionaries later because of her efforts, more educated workers better able to provide for larger families, bigger wage-earners better able to pay a greater tithing. Wiser parents better able to raise the next generation in righteousness.

Lois *was* making a difference. It wasn't enough simply to get people to join the Church, like proselytizing missionaries did. They had to be worthwhile and productive members once they were in, too.

She read one student's argument about shielding children from worldly information. "Would Nephi have been as strong a leader if he had watched the sexual freedom of 'Friends' on TV when he was a boy?"

Lois shook her head. She agreed on one level that showing promiscuity as normal and harmless was in fact very harmful, but at the same time, she wondered if Joseph Smith's legal promiscuity made him any less of a prophet. If what he had done was completely righteous, why were Mormons shielded even from the information that some of Joseph's wives also had other husbands? It seemed so often that the saints were fed milk, the Church afraid that meat would be too overpowering for them. But they couldn't stay children forever, could they?

Lois finally finished grading and went home. She was too tired to cook a good meal, but she knew Gerald would be tired as well, so she prepared a green bean casserole and a pan of brownies. She even made a fresh pitcher of Kool-Aid.

"Hi, honey, I'm home," said Gerald around 6:00, coming in the door covered on the interior with a poster of the Rexburg temple. It was a little childish to decorate with posters, something they'd never have done back home, but Lois liked feeling different than she usually did. She wanted to live like a missionary, like a young missionary.

"Gerald, you're filthy!"

"Pipe broke."

"But you don't know anything about fixing pipes."

"And a boy from Pocatello doesn't know Swahili, but we send him to Africa anyway." He grinned. "Besides, all I had to do was clean up the mess."

"Did you get everything patched up?"

"For now. It's an old building. There's always something."

"Couldn't the Church just do a renovation of some of these older properties? The Church has to face the fact that buildings grow old."

Gerald shrugged. "It's a curse being the world's fastest growing religion. We have too many meetinghouses. There's not enough money to keep them all up. That's why the Church cut the janitorial budget by 80% this year."

Lois gritted her teeth. She was so tired of hearing that statistic. The budget had been cut a full 20% only the year before. Weren't people paying their tithing? Didn't the Church have investments? Maybe they were wasting too much money on Third World countries, building churches for people whose tithing amounted to $55 a year.

But why was it Gerald's responsibility to make up the difference? Why couldn't the Church have special missionaries trained directly to entice rich people to join? Or at least to write grants to try to take in some money. What about those poor proselytizing missionaries who asked the Church pay for their missions? Perhaps the Church should require them to work for free on building projects until they made up the cost. It wasn't fair to force people who'd already worked hard their entire lives to spend their eighteen months of missionary labor mopping up dirty water. The reality of mission life just wasn't what she had expected. Why did the Church always have people talk about how incredible this time was, if it was really simply hard, mundane work? Hiding the truth only made the truth that much more appalling.

"Well, take a shower and change your clothes. Dinner will be ready in a few minutes."

Lois finished preparing the meal while Gerald cleaned up. Then they said a blessing over the food and began to eat. "So, did you have a religious experience today?" asked Lois. It was something they discussed every day, though Lois was beginning to wonder if she sounded sarcastic when she asked it.

"I always feel spiritual when I serve the Church."

"Even when you're mopping floors?"

"I think about a perfectly clean heaven."

"How about when you're cleaning toilets?"

"I think about becoming a god and never needing a toilet again."

Lois shrugged.

"Don't you feel good about serving?" asked Gerald. "Just teaching at all should be rewarding, much less teaching at a Church school."

Lois shrugged again. How was she any different from an adjunct instructor, she wondered. How was she holier? In what way was she any more helpful? Just because she saved the Church money?

"You know," said Gerald, "if we were out there preaching to Catholics in Santiago, they'd probably all be adulterers and smokers. We'd be interacting with sinners every day. Surely, it's more uplifting to be working with other saints."

Lois wondered. When she assigned topics like banning smoking in public, or closing movie theaters on Sunday, or charging higher sin taxes on alcohol, her students seemed oblivious to substantive reasoning. They were almost always for the "right" answer, but they could never effectively deal with the opposition. They seemed incapable of understanding an opponent's point of view. At first, Lois felt gratified that her students were so pure that they couldn't even conceive of a sinful position. But lately, their innocence felt less satisfying. These were adults, and they still seemed like babies. Once, Lois had used the word "penis" in class, and two days later, she was called in by the administration and chastised after a student had reported her. Lois had humbly agreed to be more careful with her word choice in the future, but she'd left the office disgusted.

Part of that was disgust at herself. The past twenty years, she'd led a sheltered life as well. She showed the kids Pixar movies, then eventually relented to a select few PG movies, but even TV shows were monitored. It was her duty to raise good, decent warriors for Zion. But now that she saw other kids like hers every day in class, she wondered if she'd made a mistake.

Lois had to read published essays on all the controversial topics she chose for class. While she'd worried at first about being struck down for reading Karl Marx or Al Gore and Bernie Sanders, something about exposing herself to radical ideas was energizing.

"We have a G.A. coming to the stake center in two weeks," said Gerald, "so I've been working extra hard getting the place up to snuff. Won't it be exciting to see a General Authority in person? We hardly ever got to see that in Omaha."

"That's true," Lois admitted. "There are definitely cultural blessings to being in Zion."

"Omaha was Zion, too," Gerald pointed out.

"But not an *important* part of Zion, or we'd have had General Authorities there, too."

Gerald shook his head. "Don't be like that, Lois. Sometimes, I think you're less righteous now than before you were a missionary."

Lois forced a smile. "Thank god I have you to bring the Spirit into our home." She said it sweetly, but Gerald gave her an odd look anyway. She looked back innocently.

She wasn't really irritated at her husband, but *something* was grating at her. She just didn't know what.

The rest of the week passed uneventfully, and Lois had all her papers for the week graded before the end of Friday afternoon. She taught five days a week, so Saturday was her P-day. Gerald usually tried to take his Preparation Day at the same time, but since he was always on call, it didn't happen every week.

Lois felt another wave of annoyance flash over her on Saturday morning when she contemplated her day. Laundry and grocery shopping were in store, plus a visit to the library to email friends and family. Why couldn't she have been sent to London like so many of the early missionaries? There were museums and art galleries there. She knew that movies, even Disney films, were off limits for missionaries, but she wished she could see a Broadway show. Omaha had felt pretty small-world, but Rexburg was even smaller. At least if she'd gone to Venezuela, there would be local culture to absorb. She wished she could see the murals of Pompeii and Herculaneum, even if they did show nudity. She'd so hoped this mission would finally give her the world.

Thinking such thoughts, of course, brought on feelings of guilt. Lois was here to serve God. It wasn't the point of a mission to have an extended vacation, or even an extended cultural experience. Missionaries had a purpose—to teach and serve. They weren't there to learn.

But did service have to be so…boring?

If only they had warned her beforehand of the reality, she could have been prepared.

Saturday afternoon, as always, Lois and Gerald went through the temple. They might as well serve the dead as the living. The dead must wonder every day why no one had prepared them for the reality of the spirit world. But dedicated saints like her were bringing them the ordinances as fast as they could.

Still, something about the way it was set up irritated Lois. Why was it *her* responsibility to do these ordinances? If there were no righteous people to do them, would all those spirits in the Spirit World just be screwed? Lois followed along with the endowment ceremony, afraid to fall asleep during the boring parts in case the spirit she was proxy for needed to see and hear through her senses, but the repetition irritated her.

Why was she irritated about everything all the time?

On Sunday, Lois and Gerald sat in Sacrament meeting and listened to others giving short talks on faith and repentance and obeying the commandments. It was the same thing every single week, month after month, year after year. Couldn't anyone talk about the biological aspects of translation? Or the physics of traveling in a beam of light? Or the chemistry of turning the Nile to blood?

No. Because they were fed pablum all the time.

Here she was in a Mormon college town, a center of learning, and she was still being treated like a child. They all were.

Is that why Glenn Beck always seemed like a brat throwing a tantrum, because Mormons were continually kept at the level of infants, to "protect" them?

Lois prepared sandwiches for lunch. She knew most Mormons liked elaborate, special meals to celebrate the

Sabbath, but she always felt that the commandment not to work on Sunday was more important, so she made her simplest meal of the week on this day. Gerald had never complained.

"Lois, you seem in one of your moods again," said Gerald softly. "It seems to happen more and more since we came to Idaho."

Lois put down her sandwich. "Gerald, why can't we ever learn about how God manipulated evolution to create us?"

"What?"

"Why can't we ever learn about how God manages the gospel on other worlds? Is there a Savior for each planet?"

"We're only given as much as we can handle now. We can't take on the mysteries of the universe before we master the basics."

Lois's jaw tensed. "That's like telling a college student there's no need to read Dostoevsky until he masters the alphabet. At *some* point, we have to grow up."

Gerald shook his head. "We have all eternity for that. Earth life is just our childhood. There's no need to grow up too fast, like those 10-year-old girls wearing make-up. We should enjoy our time here. Enjoy our childhood."

"Even children don't want to repeat the first grade endlessly. Besides, I thought the pre-existence was our childhood. We're in our adolescence now. And adolescents need a chance to grow."

Gerald shook his head again. "No. We're children who have to learn adult responsibilities by doing our chores. And I'm here to do my chores."

He seemed annoyed now, too. He got up, threw the rest of his sandwich away, and went to sit on a folding chair he carried outside.

Lois wanted to slap him.

But what had he done wrong? Why was she mad?

Lois sat on the bed, reading from the Book of Mormon. It felt like empty words, but she was going to stick with it until her heart softened and she put herself right with God again.

Then the phone rang.

"Gerald," she said a moment later, opening the door. "The sewer's backed up at church. They need you over there."

Gerald nodded and picked up his chair. As he was getting ready to leave a few minutes later, Lois started singing softly, "I hope they call me on a mission, when I have grown a foot or two."

Gerald didn't kiss her on his way out. He simply said, "I'm going to have to talk to the mission president about your attitude. Maybe he can think of something."

Lois was irritated all over again. He was treating her like a naughty child who'd stolen from the cookie jar. "How do you solve a problem like Maria?" she sang listlessly to the empty apartment.

Well, maybe she was in fact behaving petulantly. She wasn't enjoying her negative attitude. And what was the point of being rebellious if you couldn't enjoy it?

Lois put down her scriptures. They required too much thought. Instead, she picked up her latest Enola Holmes mystery. This was a series for 11- to 12-year-olds, about Sherlock Holmes's sister solving mysteries Sherlock couldn't.

Lois liked to read children's books, especially those with female protagonists. She felt a little guilty doing it on her mission, when she was only supposed to read Church literature. But reading *The Secret Garden* and *Black Beauty* was a little like listening to the Carpenters or John Denver. It wasn't the Mormon Tabernacle Choir, but it wasn't far off. And Lois felt that as an English teacher, she had to read *some* kind of literature.

As she had raised her children over the years, Lois found her attention span shortening. She could no longer read Shakespeare or, God forbid, Dickens. But she could reread all the Laura Ingalls Wilder books. They stood up well to the test of time. Lois *wanted* to read something more substantial, and it irritated her that she was reduced to reading at a sixth-grade level, but watching Laura Ingalls plot to cover Nellie Olson with leeches wasn't entirely innocent, either. And the disdain Laura felt for Mary, who calmly licked her lollipop while Laura ate hers voraciously, was clear. There was a lot to be read between the lines.

Just before coming on her mission, Lois had read *The Sweetness at the Bottom of the Pie*. It wasn't exactly a children's book, though the protagonist was an 11-year-old girl, a chemist who antagonizes her sister by putting poison ivy extract in her lipstick. Lois almost felt like an adult again reading it.

But she'd reverted back to legitimate juvenile literature when she accepted her call to serve. She absolutely loved the Theodosia Throckmorton series, reading each book twice. Then she'd decided to try the Enola Holmes series.

Theodosia had dealt with Egyptian black magic, something decent Latter-day Saints shouldn't entertain, much less missionaries. The books had even dealt with the murder of one of the villains by another villain, a bit dark for 11-year-olds, Lois thought. Nancy Drew might have to face lots of threats, but hers were pretty innocent books, after all.

But Enola Holmes...

Lois was already almost through the book, and she finished it now within about half an hour. Not only did *The Case of the Bizarre Bouquets* talk about feces in the streets of 1889 London, but there was also mention of prostitution, and the villain turned out to be a lesbian whose nose was eaten away by rats, who murdered her sister's husband. Sheesh.

Children's books weren't what they used to be. It seemed like such a loss of innocence. Lois missed the carefree days when she was a child, and it didn't seem she'd ever be able to recapture them. It seemed—

Lois sat up straight.

A loss of innocence. Facing mature topics head-on. Perhaps that was a *good* thing.

You didn't want your kids to be afraid of trick-or-treating, but you didn't want them to be poisoned, either. You didn't want your children afraid to go to the park, but you had to warn them about predators at a very early age. As soon as they were old enough to talk, you had to teach them to say, "He's not my Daddy!" if some strange man were carrying them off. Just a screaming kid was no reason to be alarmed. You had to teach your kids the exact right thing to say.

Was the whole world simply more corrupt now?

Even if it were, that was all the more reason you had to prepare children for the reality of what was actually out there.

Gerald came home from work around 6:30. Lois had prepared chicken-fried steak with rice and gravy.

"What's up?" said Gerald in confusion. "It's Sunday."

"If you can work on the Sabbath, I guess I can, too."

"But I'm serving the Church."

"And I'm serving a missionary."

Gerald smiled uncertainly but washed up and sat eagerly down to dinner.

"How was your afternoon, dear?" asked Lois.

"Okay." He still looked confused. "How was yours? Anything special planned for the coming week?"

Lois took a bite of steak and chewed while she thought about her answer. She'd decided earlier that her next essay assignment at the university would be a little different. Rather than allow the students to choose their own side of the argument, Lois was going to treat the class like a debate club. She'd force the students to take the side they would normally never choose, force them to think outside the box. She'd assign a topic like, "Why pornography is beneficial to society" or "Why profanity should be allowed on network television."

What was the Church going to do, after all? Fire her?

Well, they might. It was called excommunication. Somehow, the adventure that might follow such a thing didn't frighten her. She swallowed her mouthful of meat and smiled.

"I'm a service missionary," she said demurely. "I'm going to start actually serving my students."

Gerald smiled, too. "That's the spirit, Lois. I knew you'd grow into this calling eventually. Now we can really enjoy the rest of our mission."

They finished the remainder of their meal, chattering happily. Lois had a gleam in her eye that she hadn't had in a long while. She listened as Gerald told her about his afternoon in the meetinghouse, but she couldn't wait till the dishes were done so she could get back to her next Gilda Joyce novel, and prepare for the next meeting with her students. Those like Shawn seemed ready for a little push toward adulthood. Maybe there *was* hope, if she acted like an adult herself.

Perhaps God had done the right thing, after all, to send her to the heart of Zion. She could be a real missionary here and perform a real service.

She smiled and handed Gerald a brownie.

Tilly the Barbarian

"You seem like a real geek, Andrew," said Ryker, leaning over Andrew's desk at lunch. "Want to join me and my friends for a game of Heroquest tomorrow night?"

"Excuse me?" said Andrew. He wasn't used to other people at work talking to him socially. Ryker had begun working here just a month ago, though, and had already made several attempts at conversation. Since Ryker wasn't Mormon, of course, and smoked as well, Andrew had been polite but distant.

"Come on. You must know what people are saying about you," said Ryker, smiling pleasantly.

"Not really." Did people actually notice him enough to include him in their gossip? It was a little flattering really.

"They say you're a social misfit," Ryker continued. "And I have three other misfits coming to my house tomorrow to participate in a role-playing game. We're all just weird enough that you might like us. What do you say?"

Andrew frowned. He'd seen Ryker's wedding ring, and a photo of a woman on the man's desk. He must not be gay, though from the little experience Andrew had, getting together to play games seemed a pretty gay thing to do. Maybe geeks and gays were overlapping categories. Andrew was thirty, still single because he wasn't sure he could face an entire lifetime with a woman, but he was still a virgin as well, because he didn't want to face an eternity with demons and devils, either.

But life did get pretty lonely at times. Some days, he felt like a caveman trying to integrate into the modern world, always feeling out of place, never able to adapt as well as those cavemen in the Geico commercials on TV.

"Sure," Andrew said slowly. "It sounds like fun."

It really didn't. But what would it hurt to give it one simple try?

"Great. We usually start at 6:00 and go on until 10:00." Ryker gave Andrew the address. "It's pot luck. Can you bring some soda?"

"No problem." Andrew was already regretting his decision. Four hours? It seemed a bit much for a work night. But he was committed now, and he always kept his commitments, as any gentleman would do. He smiled and shook Ryker's hand, and then he got back to work. Throughout the rest of the day, he stole glances at Ryker, who was busily working at his own desk and ignoring Andrew. And he checked the internet every once in a while for the latest news. A terrorist train bombing in Russia. A bomb in a Pakistani mosque. But no soldiers killed in Afghanistan today. Thank god for that.

It was Monday, so that night after dinner, Andrew headed over to Melanie's apartment for the Single Adult Family Home Evening at 7:00. Mormons, of course, devoted every Monday night to family activities, but since the Singles had no families, the Church grouped them together so they would both have a spiritual experience during the week and also keep in mind that the ultimate goal was marriage and family. Andrew enjoyed being with the others, though he was getting to be much older now than the core group in their early twenties. Then, too, the knowledge that he might forever be denied a family because of his condition was becoming more and more painful to bear. But like always, he smiled and pretended to have a good time.

"Did you hear what happened to Drena?" asked Melanie once the group was all gathered and had offered an opening prayer.

"What?" asked Scott. "I wondered why she wasn't here."

Melanie leaned forward and whispered loudly, "She's been disfellowshipped for petting with a guy from work."

Everyone gasped, and half the group laughed. "Well, she was always dressing inappropriately," said Candace.

"Why didn't she ever make out with *me*?" asked Ron, laughing.

"'Cause you didn't go on a mission."

"And her coworker did?"

The group continued bantering for several minutes before the lesson started, this one about the importance of reading the scriptures daily. Andrew felt vaguely uneasy about the gossip, as always. They all loved Drena, obviously, but there still seemed to be something rather brutal about the talk.

After the lesson, they all played Charades for an hour, and then the group broke up and went their separate ways. Andrew arrived back at his place just after 9:30. Tonight's activities had lasted only two and a half hours, and he was still exhausted. He didn't know if he could handle the following evening. Maybe he should cancel.

"Andrew," said Ryker on Tuesday when he stopped by Andrew's desk during lunch. "About tonight."

Andrew smiled. Maybe he was being uninvited. Perhaps someone in Ryker's group was calling in sick.

"It looks like we really need a barbarian in our game. We already have a wizard and an elf and a dwarf. But if you agree to be a barbarian, you can be any race you choose."

Andrew frowned. "You mean, I can be Filipino?" Ryker laughed, a beautiful, hearty laugh. "I mean, you can be human or orc or a dwarf."

"Dwarves aren't human?"

Ryker laughed again. "You'll catch on before long. Why don't you start out as a human?"

Andrew nodded, and Ryker went on his way. Andrew felt like a monster most of the time because of his depravity. Maybe playing a human would help.

As long as he could avoid falling in love with Ryker. Andrew knew it was hopeless, that Ryker was straight, and that in any event, Andrew was committed to living a gospel-centered life. But he felt a tingle now as he remembered that laugh. He hoped he wasn't making a mistake.

Andrew picked up some diet root beer on his way to Ryker's house. It was a modest home in a working-class neighborhood. Andrew arrived at five minutes to 6:00. He hated being late. Tardiness was so crass.

"Buddy! Come on in!" said Ryker at the door, giving him a hug.

What was that all about?

"Andrew, this is my wife, Kelly. Kelly, this is my coworker, Andrew."

"I've heard so much about you."

Andrew laughed. "I seriously doubt it."

"Well…"

"Come on in the dining room. We'll get set up."

Andrew put his sodas on the kitchen counter and then joined Ryker around a large table covered with a tan tablecloth. There was a paper playing board set out, which simply contained a pattern of squares, and at the head of the table was a thin cardboard partition that said Overlord. Andrew hoped he wasn't getting into anything Satanic. There were lots of dice, and a handful of little plastic figurines.

A few minutes later, the doorbell rang, and another man walked in without waiting for permission to enter. "Hey, Maddock. This is Andrew."

"Nice to meet you."

"You, too," said Andrew.

"Maddock's a wizard."

Andrew didn't know how to respond to that and finally managed, "How nice for you."

Maddock laughed. "You were right about this one, Ryker."

So they had talked about him? Andrew felt his ears burn, but the guys didn't seem mean-spirited. If they didn't like him, why would they have invited him?

Perhaps he was here to provide jokes later after he was gone?

A moment later, another man walked in, more handsome than the others. Andrew suddenly felt nervous.

"Hey, Gavin. This is Andrew, the guy I was telling you about."

Gavin gave Andrew a surprisingly brazen appraisal. "Can I sit next to him?"

"No footsie under the table," said Maddock.

Andrew's whole face was burning now. "Gavin's our token queer," explained Ryker. "And we thought he could use some company."

"What do you mean, company?" asked Andrew, trying not to stutter.

"Oh, don't worry. You don't have to sleep with him unless we do a Saturday evening session that goes on all night."

Andrew was mortified.

"So how are those baby plans coming along?" asked Maddock, thankfully allowing Andrew time to recover.

"The doctor says my vasectomy may be reversible," said Ryker, "but if not, we may have to go in with a needle and extract some sperm."

"Ouch."

"How's Carol's pregnancy coming along?"

"The morning sickness is getting better."

Gavin nudged Andrew. "Breeders," he muttered, rolling his eyes.

Andrew didn't know what shocked him the most. The casual talk of heterosexual sex, the casual talk of homosexuality, or the casual acceptance that the straight men had for the gays. Or the shock that his own orientation had been so apparent.

Teague showed up a couple of minutes later. Everyone was in their early to mid-thirties. Andrew instantly felt a new level of comfort despite all the audacious talk. And it was nice they were all guys, even if…well, Andrew didn't know if it was the gay man or the straight men who were more challenging to accept.

Just before the game began, there was another scandalous moment almost too great to bear. "What would you like to name your character?" asked Ryker.

Andrew hadn't thought about it. How much could he allow himself to play? Could he name his character Arnold after Schwarzenegger? He looked about at his fellow players. Even the humans in the room had more interesting names than Andrew did. He was just a boring, boring person.

"Ralph?" he asked, feeling downright stupid.

"No," said Gavin. "Let's name him Tilly." The others all laughed, and Andrew's character was named for him. He was mortified at the effeminate name, and yet despite his burning ears, Andrew felt a little thrill as well. What would the Single Adults group think if they knew? The thought was funny at first but then quickly became sobering.

As the group looked for traps and treasure and fought zombies and other creatures, Andrew tried not to be shocked any further. But Maddock's male wizard was named Scarlet and spoke like a Southern belle, even though Maddock was supposedly straight. All the other players spoke in their character's voices, acting out entire scenarios at length. It struck Andrew as silly, and yet he envied the freedom these guys seemed to feel and luxuriate in.

The evening wore on, and Andrew found himself laughing at the jokes the others were telling. Maddock had blue balls because his wife was no longer interested in sex while pregnant. He joked about beating off while fantasizing about Ryker's wife. Then there was banter about Ryker not being a real man because of his vasectomy. But there was no cattiness, no meanness associated with the joking. At the end of the game, Teague's dwarf was killed, and Maddock's wizard pulled a card which gave him an elixir of life to bring back one dead comrade. The elixir was a "pearly white liquid" to be applied to the character's face. Everyone howled, and even Andrew understood the implications.

"Straight men have all the fun," said Gavin wistfully.

"I don't know," said Teague. "You guys get to do this in real life."

The audacity, the depravity, the sinfulness, the baseness of such talk was shocking, but even these straight married men who weren't sinning at all in their sex lives were joking as if this were nothing. It was all so confusing.

Soon, too soon, the evening was over, and yet the surprises continued as all four men hugged Andrew good-bye. Mormons always shook hands, which Andrew loved, because non-members so often didn't have any physical contact at all, but these guys hugged. Were they really straight? Maybe they'd done as he was contemplating, married women they weren't attracted to. But if they were this accepting of homosexuality, why would they have bothered? Was it simply that non-members didn't understand the gravity of the situation? Perhaps he should stay away from them, after all.

Andrew went home, checked the news for the latest from Afghanistan, and read another chapter in the Book of Mormon.

When he grew tired of that, he kneeled beside his bed to pray. "Please don't let me be corrupted," he begged wearily. He climbed into bed and smiled weakly, despite his worries. It had been a fun evening.

Ryker was friendly to Andrew at work, though their paths didn't directly cross very often throughout the day. He made a point of assuring Andrew the other players liked him and wanted him to return the following Tuesday. Andrew agreed, still unsure what was best.

Saturday night was a Singles dance at the stake center. Andrew went and asked a few of the less attractive girls to dance. They didn't look any more excited about it than he did.

Church on Sunday went as usual. It was Andrew's turn to teach the elders quorum lesson. He wasn't much of a teacher, going straight from the manual. The class naturally found it boring, but what was he to do? The bishop had called him to the position, and no matter how unqualified Andrew actually was, he had to do his duty. It would be uncivilized not to.

The only interesting part of the lesson came near the end, when Andrew stumbled over part of the material, and there was a long moment of silence. Tony, the second counselor in the elders quorum, took the opportunity to make an unrelated comment. "Hey, did everyone hear what's going on in Uganda?"

"No."

"What?"

"They're proposing a new law that will sentence gays to death. And anyone who knows of a gay person will get three years in prison if they don't report that person to the authorities."

"All right!"

"About time."

"Doesn't that seem too extreme?" This comment came from Edward, who was married with two kids.

"These guys are trying to destroy marriage. They'll take us back to the Stone Age."

"There were gays in the Stone Age?"

"You know what I mean. Gays want to destroy civilization."

"Well, maybe if the law passes, and other countries don't protest, the world will see that no one cares, and other places can follow suit."

"Homosexuals just want to reduce us to animals."

"There are gay animals?" asked Andrew, biting his lip for joining in the discussion when he still had other points the manual wanted him to make.

"All I'm saying is we ought to consider harsher penalties in this country. You saw the latest poll? Utah ranks lowest in the nation in attitudes toward gay rights."

"You have that backward. Utah is first in the nation in support of righteousness."

"The bottom line is that gays are trying to destroy the Church, and God will never allow it. He'll wipe them out one way or another."

The talk threatened to go on, but Andrew forced himself to clear his throat loudly. "*Anyway,*" he said, trying to regain control of his class, "the next point of the lesson, if you'll turn the page…" The elders had clearly been more interested in this topical argument than in Andrew's lesson, but Andrew couldn't bear to hear the hatred in their voices. They would cut him out of their lives in a heartbeat if they knew his secret. How could he ever feel the brotherhood of the Church, knowing these people despised him?

Andrew's mind wandered more than usual during Sunday School and Sacrament meeting. In some ways, the Church had grown more understanding toward homosexuality over the years, he reflected. But as last year's Proposition 8 in California had proven, the Church and its members still hated gays, despite whatever "gentle" phrases they might try to use. Maybe he was contaminating himself by playing with Ryker and his friends on Tuesday. The battle was hard enough when he was pure. He'd never manage it with an evil spell cast over him.

Andrew spent the rest of the day reading a book by Boyd K. Packer and then watching *The Other Side of Heaven*. He felt better by the time he went to bed.

Andrew determined the next day to tell Ryker he couldn't make the Tuesday night meeting, yet somehow, they never seemed to run into each other all day, and Andrew was left with the commitment to say something first thing the following morning.

Monday night was Family Home Evening again at Melanie's apartment. Drena was there this time, and everyone acted happy to see her. She was frank about her recent troubles, admitting to spending the night with her boyfriend. "But we broke up," she said. "I guess I kind of provoked it, in order to save my character."

"What did you do?" asked Candace.

"Well, he had this horrible monkey. It was always masturbating."

Everyone laughed nervously.

"And it threw feces all the time."

"Ugh."

"He had it in the back yard in its cage during the daytime last Saturday. But he forgot to bring it in at night because he was distracted by my sleeping over. I remembered the monkey, but I hated it, so I left it outside. And of course, you remember how cold it got last weekend." She shrugged. "The monkey was dead by morning."

There were a couple of gasps, followed by laughter. Andrew, though, was appalled. Drena had killed a living creature just to break up with her boyfriend? Even if she'd done it simply out of hatred for the animal itself, nothing seemed an adequate justification. How could everyone be laughing about it like it was merely a naughty prank?

The group settled down shortly and they had a lesson on the importance of prayer. Then they played Pictionary, and everyone went home.

Andrew lay in bed a long while, thinking.

The next morning when his alarm went off, Andrew thought about calling in sick to work. But that wouldn't be right, so he got dressed and ate a quick breakfast. He avoided Ryker for most of the morning, but during lunch, Ryker stopped by Andrew's desk.

"How's Tilly doing?"

"Oh, uh, um, just fine."

"So we're still on for tonight?"

"Sure."

"Great. Gavin will be pleased."

With that, Ryker left, and Andrew had to figure out what he meant by his comment. Was Gavin interested in him? Should Andrew change his mind and cancel in order to protect himself from temptation? Perhaps Gavin simply liked not being the lone gay man in attendance. Andrew knew what it was like to be all alone. He always felt like a loathsome bug at church. But maybe Gavin just liked him as a friend. It would be nice to have a real friend, wouldn't it?

There wasn't time to worry about it too much, though. There was plenty of work to do, and Andrew barely had time to check Yahoo for news just once around 4:00. There was a shooting in Michigan, and a reference to the fact that Utah was the only state that allowed guns on school campuses. Two soldiers were killed in a helicopter crash in Afghanistan. Andrew's heart skipped a beat, as it did every time he heard bad news from the region. He hoped that Steven was okay.

Andrew barely even knew Steven. The man was seven years younger than he was. Andrew had sent him a couple of encouraging letters when Steven was a missionary in Sweden. It wasn't till he came home, looking like a real man for the first time, that Andrew had really sat up straight to take a good look. He tried to befriend the young man in the Single Adults program but not two months after he returned to the States, Steven had joined the Army, and now he was stationed in Afghanistan, fighting the evil Taliban.

Part of Andrew admired Steven for it. But part of him hated that the man was forced to live in the desert in a Third World country where the literacy rate was only 10%. Part of him felt that unchecked, terrorists could precipitate World War III. But part of him also felt that aggression on our part was only exacerbating the problem. Why did people like to fight so much anyway? Why did grown men like Ryker and Gavin think *pretending* to fight every Tuesday was a fun pastime? It almost seemed insulting to be playing a game of pretend heroism while Steven was facing bullets and roadside bombs every day. Maybe tonight should be Andrew's last time.

Andrew brought cans of diet crème soda tonight, and shortly after 6:00, the gang was all seated, ready to play. "The doctor *is* going to have to use a needle to get my sperm," Ryker announced.

"Barbaric," muttered Teague.

"What's barbaric is living with a pregnant wife," said Maddock, putting his hand to his forehead. "I wish some of these spells in my bag were real."

"That's advanced gaming," said Ryker. "We're not ready for that yet."

Everyone laughed except Andrew, who was afraid again he was getting in over his head in some kind of witchcraft. "Look, guys, I'm Mormon," he said abruptly, his heart beating hard. "I don't know if I feel comfortable playing."

"You're Mormon?" asked Gavin. "Hey, did I ever tell you guys about when I took a tour of the Mormon temple here before they opened it? Apparently, heathens are only allowed to see the place before it's 'dedicated,' and then only card-carrying Mormons can go in after that. Is that right, Andrew?"

Andrew nodded uncertainly.

"Anyway, I went in with all these stickers that said, 'Gay Christians have met here,' and I put them everywhere. I put them underneath vases, under chairs and sofas, insider drawers, underneath toilet lids, absolutely every place I could think of."

Andrew's mouth fell open in horror.

"Then when I got home, I called the temple and told them what I'd done. I said I'd placed one hundred stickers, but I really only placed ninety-one. I figured they'd tear the place up looking for those last nine."

Everyone howled, and as horrifying as the story was, Andrew found himself slightly impressed.

"Speaking of barbaric, they said what I'd done was a vicious vandalism, and they threatened to prosecute me. But the temple was dedicated on schedule, and the world didn't seem to come to an end."

"It was a lot like after Prop 8," said Ryker. "The Mormons went on and on about all the 'violence' they suffered, which amounted to a couple of cans of spray paint."

"But...but..." Andrew spluttered.

"I understand," said Gavin softly. "I read Patty Hearst's autobiography. I know how brain washing can turn even a respectable person into a criminal."

Andrew's mouth fell open again. Had Gavin really said such an outrageous thing? He completely disapproved of what Gavin had done, and yet as a brutal act, it hardly compared to what was going on in Uganda. Andrew had been reading the Church website and following the news. No major religious or political leaders in America were condemning the proposed law. Why wasn't the prophet denouncing it? The gospel was supposed to bring a civilizing influence upon the world. Was it just "not their problem"? The Church avoided speaking on "political" issues, but if gay marriage was a "moral" issue here in the U.S., then why wasn't the murder of gays a moral issue as well? But tonight, instead of feeling like a worm, thinking about his position in the universe just made Andrew angry.

He behaved recklessly throughout the game, opening doors without checking for traps, being the first to engage monsters in battle, letting the others gather all the treasure. He felt he'd given up before even starting, and that made the game not as fun as it had been last week. And yet part of him enjoyed the recklessness, too.

"Andrew's really getting into this," said Maddock.

"If he gets hurt much more in battle," said Gavin, "he may need some special comforting later."

Teague laughed. "But you don't have any healing spells."

"I've got some pearly white liquid left over."

"Left over from what?" asked Ryker, smiling.

"I beat off in your bathroom every Tuesday night, listening to your sexy voice through the door."

"Well, *I* beat off in your bathroom every Tuesday night, too," said Maddock, "listening to *Kelly's* voice through the door."

Andrew put his dice down and stood up.

"You okay?" asked Ryker.

Andrew was trembling. He knew this was a pivotal moment in his life, and he had to be strong. What he wanted was *everyone's* leftover sperm. But he was going to be good. He was going to be civilized. He was going to be a light set on a hill.

"I can't come here anymore."

There was only a brief moment of surprised silence before Gavin said, "We're compromising his virtue. I've seen it before."

"Is there a cure?" asked Maddock.

"Anyone got a spell?"

Ryker, who was sitting just to the right of Andrew, at the head of the table, stood up. "I don't know if I have any potions specifically designed to eradicate this problem, but I do have a magic wand." Without another word, he unzipped his pants and pulled out his penis.

There was immediate laughter around the table.

"Finally!" said Gavin. "I've been coming over here for ages waiting to see that."

"Well, I could live without the images I'll have to deal with when I go to sleep tonight," said Teague, "but…" He stood up and unzipped as well, pulling out his member.

Then Maddock and Gavin followed suit. Andrew watched in horror-struck fascination. The straight guys all had flaccid penises, but Gavin's was half-erect. What kind of friends would stand around doing such a thing? What kind of animals were they? The men were all pointing at each other and laughing, as if this were nothing, all except Gavin, who was just looking and smiling pleasantly.

"Come on, Andrew, your turn."

Andrew would *never* be so vulgar as to show his penis in public, and yet part of him sensed the camaraderie the others were feeling, and he longed to experience that. And part of him just wanted to be wild and dangerously lawless. And part of him wanted Gavin to see him and like what he saw.

He slowly unzipped and pulled out his fully erect penis.

"Not bad," said Gavin.

"Are you kidding?" said Maddock. "How can I possibly seduce Kelly now, seeing what I'm up against with *all* you guys?"

"Whose turn is it?" said Ryker. "Maddock, I think you're up." With that, everyone zipped their pants and got back to the game. Andrew sat down again as well, confused. He didn't want to leave anymore. They continued playing till about 9:45, and then everyone hugged, and Andrew drove home in silence.

It took him a long while to fall asleep.

Ryker stopped by during lunch the next day to say hi. Andrew brought his Book of Mormon to work for the rest of the week and read it during his breaks each day.

Saturday night was movie night with the Singles. They met at Melanie's for 8:00 to pop some popcorn and watch *The Rock*. "Nobody tell the bishop we're watching an R-rated movie," said Ron.

"Speaking of R ratings," said Drena, "did you hear about Steven?"

Andrew sat up straight and stared at Drena. "What?" Had he been hurt? Or—

"He got kicked out of the Army for being gay."

268

"No!"

"Really?"

The others laughed. "I always thought he was too prissy to carry a gun."

"Wasn't he nominated for Soldier of the Year? What a joke."

"He only joined so he could take showers with other guys."

"I wonder how many soldiers he's tried to rape? He's probably raping Afghani civilians, ruining our international relations."

Andrew stared at his friends in shock. They had been praising Steven's patriotism just two weeks before. What kind of loyalty dissolved in mere seconds? He nodded slowly. He'd always understood that Church members would abandon him without a thought, but to see that callousness in action was sobering. He felt as if he were watching some hulking man throw a tiny dog out the window of a speeding car onto a busy freeway.

"Steven is a good man," said Andrew softly but firmly.

The others stopped and looked at him.

"I never heard *him* gossiping maliciously," Andrew continued.

Candace turned up her nose. "Well, *he* can't throw stones because *he* lives in a glass house."

For some reason, the comment really irritated Andrew. "And you live in a cave," he said coldly.

"Why are you defending Steven?" asked Ron. "Are you queer, too?"

Andrew stood up, walked to the bedroom to pick up his coat, and left without another word. Sitting in his car, he held onto the steering wheel tightly for several moments, thinking of defenseless Chihuahuas, which slowly morphed in his thoughts into mastiffs with spiked collars. Then he pulled out his cell phone and called Ryker.

"What's up, Buddy?"

"I was wondering if you had Gavin's phone number."

"Sure thing." There was no smugness or smirking tone to Ryker's voice, even though Andrew knew he must be able to connect the dots. Andrew thanked him and then took a deep breath, looking at the number in his hands.

"Hello?"

"Hi, Gavin. It's Andrew."

"Oh, hey, how are you?"

"Well, I'm thinking about next Tuesday."

"Yeah?"

"I decided my character needs a sword in addition to his axe. I'm in a fighting mood."

"What brought that on?"

"A surge of testosterone." Andrew wondered if it really did all come down to hormones. Was it his spirit or his body that was in control? "Is there a sledgehammer in the arsenal?"

Gavin laughed. "I love my men butch."

"Can I come over to your place?"

Gavin laughed again. "Sure. I just showered to get ready for the bars later, but I'd rather see you."

Andrew smiled.

"And just FYI, I douched as well."

It took Andrew a moment to figure out what Gavin meant, and then he laughed despite himself. "I'll keep that in mind."

Andrew drove a few miles over to Gavin's place, following the directions Gavin had given him over the phone. It wasn't hard to recognize the house when he arrived. There was a large two-story covered in Christmas lights, with lighted reindeer on the roof, and a large, lighted snowman in the yard. That wasn't Gavin's house, though. His was the one-story beside it, dark except for the few strings of lights on the roof spelling out the word "DITTO" and an arrow pointing to the house next door.

Andrew smiled and walked up the front path. He paused a moment, thinking of Steven and if he'd need a place to stay. Steven was certainly welcome to share Andrew's house if he wanted. It would be better, of course, if Steven's family still accepted him, but there was obviously no guarantee of that. Andrew wondered how Steven's situation would affect his own future. Would he start dating Gavin tonight only to switch to Steven a few days later? It was so confusing not to have strict guidelines confining your every move. Even Heroquest had rules. But now Andrew had to make up his own as he went along.

He knocked, and a moment later, Gavin opened the door. He was wearing high leather boots, a tunic, and a flowing, hunter green cape. "Are you a weary traveler seeking lodging for the night?" asked Gavin in an officious tone.

"Uh, yes," said Andrew.

"Well, we extend every civility to wanderers. Do come in." Gavin motioned for Andrew to enter, and he did so cautiously.

They stood looking at each other seriously for a moment, and then Gavin winked. "I thought we'd do some *real* role-playing tonight."

Andrew smiled, and Gavin grew serious again. "Our barmaid will serve you shortly, good sir, but first, let me show you to your quarters. Perhaps, for a small token of appreciation, I could arrange for you to be served in your room."

Andrew followed Gavin uncertainly, yet still smiling a little in anticipation. Gavin really was a misfit, it seemed, but he supposed he was one, too. Andrew realized with complete clarity now that he'd never fit into mainstream society. He wondered if he was starting an adventure tonight that would bring on battles against ogres and giants, and if he was even starting out on level one, but he was willing to see where the story led.

Once in the bedroom, Gavin pretended to kneel down as the host of the inn for the purpose of removing Andrew's shoes. But that game ended pretty quickly as they moved on to a new one. It turned out that the douching did come in handy, after all. Afterward, Andrew and Gavin lay on the bed cuddling. Andrew put his head on Gavin's chest, and Gavin caressed Andrew's arm lightly.

"This isn't a game, you know," said Gavin softly. "You of all people must know we have real enemies out there."

"Yes," said Andrew slowly. "But we have the Overlord on our side, don't we?"

"Even with friendly overlords, elves get shot with arrows, and dwarves get their arms hacked off. Being gay isn't only about love. It's about violence, too."

Andrew was silent a moment. "You have any more of those stickers you brought to the temple?" he finally asked.

"Yes," Gavin replied in a confused tone. "Why?"

"I still have my temple recommend. I can get back in with them again next week."

Gavin laughed. "Barbarians aren't the best undercover agents, you know."

"The Mormons are the real infiltrators, though, aren't they?"

"You sure you're up to taking them on? Prophets are like wizards. They can cast spells over people."

Andrew reflected on the statement for a moment. "I may get killed in the first round," he said slowly, "but I won't go down without a fight."

"Well, I'm up for any kiss-ins you want to participate in." Gavin squeezed Andrew's shoulder and then touched it with his lips. "Sheesh, kiss-ins," he said. "You know, the real problem here is that our attacks are a lot less brutal than theirs. When you're heartless, you can fight pretty savagely."

"Then maybe a little more barbarity on our part is in order."

Just then, Andrew felt a bite on his nipple and jumped. A moment later, Gavin bit his other nipple, too.

"Animal," said Andrew, laughing.

"You have no idea, Tilly," Gavin replied.

But Andrew was pretty sure he wanted to find out, and to unleash the animal in himself, too.

"Call me Attila," he said and smiled. Then he bared his teeth as well.

Pecking Order

"Sister Reed, would you mind taking out the trash again?" Sister Wright said sweetly, scrunching up her face with a smile. "I know it's my chore this week, but Sister Godfrey and I have a teaching appointment, and we're running a bit late." She shrugged to show her incompetence. "Do you mind terribly?" Now she put on a pained yet hopeful expression.

"No, that's fine," said Sister Reed. "I need the exercise." She smiled back, but really, she was in fact irritated. Sister Reed had done almost all of Sister Wright's and Sister Godfrey's chores all week. It was Godfrey's week to cook, for instance, but one day, she complained of cramps and asked Sister Reed to cook for her, and another day, she had suffered a bad headache and needed a substitute in the kitchen again.

Sister Wright had sweeping duty in addition to trash removal this week, and one day, she'd asked Sister Reed to do it, "so I can have more Dual Study time with my companion, so we don't lose hours just because she's sick." They always had legitimate enough reasons, but it was Sister Reed who ended up doing all the work. She didn't feel everything should be dumped on her just because she was the newest missionary in the group.

Sister Reed grabbed the plastic bag in the kitchen and headed downstairs. The sisters lived on the third floor in this apartment building in northeast Rome. Sister Pollo was from Sicily, and she enjoyed living in central Italy now, though she expressed annoyance when her accent gave her away. It seemed the further north you lived in Italy, the more respectable you were. But even with that unfair judgment placed on her, Sister

Reed noted that her companion had no trouble enjoying the privileged status of "native missionary." In the mission field, Utah Mormons ranked highest, followed by Idaho, Arizona, and then California Mormons. Missionaries like Reed from the southeastern U.S. were a distant tenth in line.

Sister Godfrey had joked once, "My name is godlike, so it's only natural I act as district leader for the sisters when the elders aren't around." Naturally, the real reason the others let her take charge was because her uncle was a General Authority, and that put her in Latter-day Saint aristocracy.

Godfrey's companion, Sister Wright, added, "And as her companion, it's only 'right' that I be second in command." She, of course, had a father who was a stake president.

That left the Italian Pollo as third, and Sister Reed ended up doing everyone else's chores half the time. It annoyed her the most when she had to clean the toilet two weeks in a row. These were missionaries, she thought. They were spiritual, righteous. Why were they behaving in such a petty way?

Perhaps it was she herself who was being petty, Reed thought, worrying about such minor faults in others.

Soon, it was 3:30 and lunch period was over, and the sisters all left the apartment at the same time. But Godfrey and Wright took the bus in one direction while Reed and Pollo went the other way.

Sisters Reed and Pollo arrived at their tracting zone shortly, and Sister Pollo handed Reed the tracting book. They kept a chart of each building they tracted, each floor in the building, and each door on the floor. That way, if no one was home, they could zero in on the right door the following day without hitting an anti-Mormon twice.

"What's the next palazzo?" asked Sister Pollo.

"This one." Sister Reed pointed.

They noticed someone leaving the building and quickly hurried in while the front door was open. There was no elevator, so the sisters climbed up five flights of stairs and knocked at the first door on the top floor, still panting.

"Chi e'?" asked a female voice from inside the apartment. The sisters waited until the door opened.

"We're from the Church of Jesus Christ—"

"I'm not interested." The woman shut her door.

Sister Pollo knocked at the next one.

"Chi e'?" asked another woman.

When the door opened, the sisters smiled pleasantly to show their spiritual glow, and Sister Pollo spoke this time. "We're representatives of the Mormon Church—"

"You're from Palermo?"

"Yes," Sister Pollo admitted cautiously.

The woman smiled. "So you went from being a Mafia wife to being the wife of a polygamist? Was that really a step up?"

"I'm not married at all. I'm a virgin."

The woman laughed.

"And no one in my family is in the Mafia."

"Uh-huh."

"We have a message about a modern day prophet we'd like to share with you," Sister Pollo went on.

The woman shook her head. "Look, you're at the bottom of the heap. Even the Jehovah's Witnesses are a rung above you. And I'm a Catholic in Rome. I like my position just fine." She closed the door.

"Why didn't you say anything?" Sister Pollo complained. "You need to contribute something, too."

Sister Reed smiled in apology, knowing her companion was really upset with the woman at the door and not her. The other sisters always seemed dissatisfied with their lack of success, and it was usually Sister Reed who took the brunt most of the time. Some days, it was all Sister Reed could do not to shout, "Repent if you want to have the Spirit!" just to see the reaction of the other sisters. But she knew she'd have been stepping out of her place to make such a comment. And the other sisters were probably more righteous than she was in any event. Some days, she wasn't even sure she had a testimony.

They kept going door to door until 7:30. No one invited them in, but just before they finished for the evening, they did manage a fifteen-minute conversation with a woman about forty in her doorway. "Look," she finally said. "What you say sounds interesting enough, but the fact is my husband would never allow me to see you. And he's the boss around here. What he says goes."

"But we live in a modern age," said Sister Reed. "You can make up your own mind. My mother did. My father never became a Mormon."

"Things are different in Italy, dear."

Sister Reed thought about it as they caught the bus and headed home. Even her mother in rural Alabama had had to agree to certain conditions in order for her father to allow her

278

and the three children to be baptized six years earlier. Her mother had always been in charge of the chickens, of course, but now she had to accept responsibility for feeding the horses as well, though horses had always terrified her. Sister Reed's mother even had to start cleaning out the stables, but she believed in the Church and did what she had to do. Her mother's faith had been infectious, but when Sister Reed had decided she wanted to serve a mission when she turned twenty-one, her father had made more demands.

"I'll support you," he said, "but that means you get nothing after this. No help getting a car, or going to school, or getting a house. No nothing. So you decide right now, young lady. You want to be a missionary, or you want to have a good life?"

"God will provide if you won't, Daddy," said Sister Reed. "I'm not at the bottom of *his* list."

Sisters Reed and Pollo were able to sit on the bus this evening for a change. Elders were never allowed to sit. The mission president felt that as crowded as Italian buses usually were, it would generate resentment if able young men took seats away from others. But the sisters were allowed to sit if seats were available. And this privilege was mitigated by other restrictions. They still had to return to their apartments by 8:00, an hour and a half earlier than the elders. They also could only serve for eighteen months against the elders' two years. They were clearly lower on the totem pole, but Sister Reed was determined to prove herself worthy, to God, to her mother, and to everyone else. Tonight, as they rode along, Sister Reed looked out the window into the dark streets, lost in thought.

Sisters Godfrey and Wright were already back in the apartment when Reed and Pollo returned. Sister Godfrey had her hair in a towel, and Sister Wright was in the bathroom washing hers. "There won't be any more hot water tonight," Sister Godfrey apologized, "unless you want to heat some on the stove."

"No, I'm okay," said Sister Reed, smiling. "*My* hair is beautiful even when it's dirty."

She didn't know why she'd proclaimed such a thing, but no one paid attention to anything she said anyway.

"Oh, I spilled some sugar on the kitchen floor when we got home," said Godfrey casually. "We're so tired after our lesson, though. Do you mind cleaning it up?"

In bed later, Sister Reed prayed. Missionary work was not what she'd expected. She'd been out six months now, and she had yet to baptize a single person. Well, naturally, she wouldn't get to baptize anyone herself. It would be the elders, the ones with the right to hold the priesthood, but she could at least turn someone over to them. And yet, she had not managed to convey the Spirit to anyone at all. Perhaps she truly was inferior. She pulled the covers to her chin and bit her lip.

Wasn't it true, though, she started to wonder, that when the zone leaders found women interested in the lessons, they always gave their referrals to Sisters Godfrey and Wright, who had the phone in their room? Naturally, they'd baptize more. Sister Reed had never been given the address of even one interested contact. And how many people did Godfrey find all by herself?

It wasn't fair. Yet obviously, Sister Reed should be able to pull her own weight regardless.

She felt like the middle child all over again. With an older sister and a younger brother, Sister Reed had faced most of her life as the least important sibling. She couldn't deny that part of her motivation for serving a mission was so perhaps she could move up to at least second place. But her older sister had married in the temple, which trumped missionary service, and her younger brother still might do both.

At least then, maybe her family would get some respect in the ward. Mixed-faith families ranked pretty low on the LDS righteousness scale.

The next morning started out with Sister Reed being fourth in line for the shower, which meant cold water again, as usual. She wondered if she had the nerve to suggest a rotating schedule but then decided the others had no incentive to vote for such a program even if she brought it up.

She just *had* to do something incredible while she was out here. Baptize a family of five. Convert a cardinal. Something.

After breakfast and Quiet Hour and Devotional, Sisters Reed and Pollo headed over to Piazza Sempione to do some 24-hour work. They stopped women in the midst of their shopping to ask them about the Church. Interrupting people was excruciating for Sister Reed, but it was part of the program, so she did it. She much preferred tracting in the evenings. People seemed to get so annoyed when they were stopped abruptly.

But today, wonderfully, fantastically, miraculously, Sister Reed was able to initiate a conversation with a woman about forty, dressed in black, who seemed receptive. "Do you think I could ever be with my husband again?" the woman asked.

"Oh, yes," said Sister Reed. "We believe in eternal marriage."

"Davvero?" She looked thoughtful. "Would you young ladies be able to come by my apartment around 1:00?"

That was an awkward time, as lunch ran from 1:30 to 3:30, but Sister Reed nodded happily and wrote down the woman's name, Anna, and her address.

"I'm the senior companion," Sister Pollo reminded her after the woman had moved on. "You really shouldn't make appointments before consulting with me."

"You have anything better to do at 1:00 today?" asked Sister Reed, feeling her face flush with irritation.

"I'm just saying. There are protocols."

The rest of the morning was still painful, full of rejection, but finally at 12:40, the sisters started over toward Anna's apartment. If the woman fed them lunch, they could get an extra two hours of work done today. They'd outshine Godfrey and Wright when it came time to turn their stats over to the zone leaders.

But there was no smell of cooking when Sisters Reed and Pollo were ushered into Anna's apartment. Still, a teaching appointment was no small thing. They were lucky to get three a week. Anna did offer them some aranciata, and then Sister Pollo started on the lesson, about Joseph Smith's First Vision. The two sisters took turns with the various Concepts, and at the end of the lesson, Sister Reed asked, "Do you have any questions?"

"Well, you mentioned earlier something about eternal marriage, but you didn't say a thing about it just now."

"That's because it's a little more advanced," said Sister Pollo. "We usually start out with the basics."

"But I want to know about *this*. What is eternal marriage?"

Sister Pollo sighed, but Sister Reed spoke right up. "A couple married in the temple can live together as husband and wife for eternity."

Anna frowned. "But my husband is dead. How can he go to the temple?"

"Sister Reed…" her companion warned.

"We do proxy work in the temple on behalf of those who have died. If the spirit in the Spirit World accepts the baptism or marriage, then it's as if they performed that ordinance themselves while alive."

Anna looked thoughtful. "So my husband can become Mormon even though he's dead?"

"That's right." Sister Reed smiled.

"But…but what if he doesn't want to marry me again?"

"He *has* to, Anna, if he wants to go to the Celestial Kingdom."

"Sister Reed…"

Anna tilted her head questioningly, and Sister Reed went on. "There are three degrees in heaven," she explained, "the Celestial, the Terrestrial, and the Telestial. The better you are in this life, the higher up you go in the next, and the more privileges you have."

"Privileges?"

Sister Reed took another sip of her orange soda. "Eternal marriage, for one. Only those who make it to the highest degree in the Celestial Kingdom get that."

Anna nodded, looking at the floor pensively. "But what about…you know…I've heard Mormons practice polygamy."

Sister Reed didn't need her companion's hand on her arm to know she was treading some dangerous water now. "We don't practice polygamy in this life," she said carefully, "though it's *possible* once we're in heaven, that a man may take on more than one wife."

Anna frowned again.

"But as the first wife, you'll always be number one," Sister Reed added quickly, hoping to soften the blow.

Yet Anna's frown deepened. "Well, how can that be?" she asked. "I would hope that at least in heaven, everyone was equal."

Sister Reed hesitated. What had Anna meant by equal? That all wives should be on the same level with each other? Or that the option to have plural spouses should be offered to women as well as to men? Or that—

Suddenly, Sister Reed fell silent, her mouth hanging open. She'd just had a revelation.

She knew, of course, that Heavenly Father had multiple wives. It was a given that for every god there were likely several goddesses. But while Sister Reed knew that her Heavenly Parents had created billions and billions of spirit children, only now had godly parentage struck her as odd.

Heavenly Father, naturally, was the father of both Lucifer and Jesus. Everyone knew that. But...but...Sister Reed wasn't sure she could face the implications which seemed so obvious now but which had never even occurred to her before.

It seemed unlikely that with so many wives, and so many offspring, that the *same* wife had given birth to these very different siblings. What if wife #4 had given birth to Lucifer, and wife #16 had given birth to Jesus? How *could* there be equality in heaven? How could you treat the woman who'd brought so much grief to the world the same as the woman who'd saved it?

And what of all the other wives who'd just had average children? Did they move up and down the ranks as various offspring became prophets or apostates? "I have 397,462 kids that have their calling and election made sure. How many have *you* got?"

Something wasn't adding up.

"Sister Reed?" asked Anna. "Are you all right?"

"I don't feel very well. Perhaps we should leave."

Sister Pollo offered a brief prayer, and then the sisters shook Anna's hand and headed out of the building. "What's wrong?" asked Sister Pollo.

Sister Reed didn't answer but walked directly to the bus stop. She looked about her at the other pedestrians, some dressed nicely and others clearly of a lower class. Some seemed refined, others tacky or trashy.

This was all surely a result of the world's fallen status. And it would naturally still exist even in the lower orders of heaven. But gods were perfect. How could you have one perfect being at a higher level than another perfect being?

And yet, wouldn't Heavenly Father always be *her* god even if she reached godhood herself? Wouldn't there *always* be some line of authority to follow? The whole Church was based, after all, on a belief in hierarchy.

And what about the scripture that promised, "The first shall be last and the last shall be first"? There might be a *reversal* of status, but there was still obviously status itself.

Sister Reed wondered if she was simply misguided because she was American and had been indoctrinated by worldly ideas of equality. Perhaps equality wasn't even a gospel principle to begin with. Was she going to let national cultural dogma outrank her religious beliefs?

A bus pulled up to the stop a few minutes later, and the sisters climbed on board. It was crowded for lunchtime, so Sister Reed grabbed a bar and held on. An unattractive man in his mid-twenties smiled shyly at her and offered his seat. Sister Reed smiled weakly back and shook her head. Then she had another revelation, right there on the bus. She put her hand on the young man's arm and nodded, trying a mixture of friendliness with the slightest hint of flirtatiousness. The man's eyes lit up, and he smiled happily to have been acknowledged. Making the young man feel more attractive by taking his seat was the least she could do, Sister Reed thought, even if the feeling only lasted a few moments.

Sister Pollo gave Sister Reed a concerned glance, but Sister Reed knew what she had to do from now on. It wasn't only a matter of being nice to the downtrodden she casually ran across. It wasn't even a matter of putting uppity people in their place. She was fighting now for the proletariat of the Spirit World, fighting against the bourgeoisie of the afterlife.

There were, after all, only two possibilities. Either the prophets had gotten the details wrong, or the facts themselves were unacceptable. Yet the prophets had reasoned with God in the Old Testament, gotten him to change his mind about various plans. So she was going to do the same.

Perhaps God had no incentive to do away with a system that kept him permanently on top of billions of other beings, but the French had overthrown their aristocracy, hadn't they? The Russians had as well. The Russian communists might be viewed as evil, but the democratic French were still seen as heroes.

And now the lowly daughter of an Alabama farmer was going to take on God. She was going to be a hero, too.

As the sisters exited the bus, Sister Reed walked back to the apartment with more assurance than usual, her head lifted higher.

"You're late," said Sister Godfrey accusingly when the two walked into the apartment. "Lunch is over, but you still have to do the dishes."

Sister Reed said nothing but instead pulled out a large bowl and filled it with water. She walked to Godfrey and Wright's bedroom, set the bowl on the floor near the bed, and sat down on the edge of the bed to remove her shoes. Sisters Godfrey and Wright watched in confusion, but then Sister Reed pointed imperiously at Sister Wright. "You," she said, "wash my feet." The two American sisters gaped, while Sister Pollo tried to follow the conversation in English. "And you," said Sister Reed, pointing to Godfrey, "take a letter to your uncle."

There was a no-nonsense tone to her voice, and the sisters actually obeyed despite their irritation.

"I've had a revelation," Sister Reed said confidently. The others all looked at her with awed reverence. Revelation out-trumped everything, even if girls weren't normally supposed to be prophets. "And there are going to be a few changes around here."

Then, as she composed her letter, Sister Reed let the others know just what those changes would be.

Also by Johnny Townsend

Dinosaur Perversion

God's Gargoyles

Mormon Underwear

Sex Among the Saints

The Circumcision of God

Available for order at BookLocker.com, or from your favorite online or neighborhood bookstore.